Praise for

SOMEBODIES
AND NOBODIES

I've been disturbed, especially during the past several years,
by my restaurant encounters. The servers invariably wear an ID:
Barbara or James. I, as patron, am always addressed with the prefix
"Mr." I've always made a point to ask, "What's your last name?"
I'm not out to make trouble, just curious. The server then often
mumbles, as though embarrassed, his or her surname.

Consider this a metaphor for the theme of Robert Fuller's
wonderful and tremendously important book on the "ism" that is
far more encompassing than racism, sexism or ageism. "Rankism"
must be our prime target from now on in. Viva Fuller!

— Studs Terkel, Pulitzer Prize-winning author of *Working* and *The Good War*

Whether it's because of race, religion, gender, class, title, or age,
abuses of rank have impeded our attempt to create social justice.
Robert Fuller's exploration of how we use and abuse rank,
both personally and politically, could help change that.

— Betty Friedan, author of *The Feminine Mystique* and *The Fountain of Age*, founder of
National Organization for Women.

Robert Fuller is a witness for invisibles everywhere who have
failed to reach their highest potential because their gifts come
in packages not considered worthy of time or attention.
His steady beam of respect has inspired us — two former
nobodies — to create The Dignitarian Foundation
<Dignitarians.org>, whose purpose is to make the invisibles visible.

— Ann and Mary Lou Richardson, co-founders of The Dignitarian Foundation

Robert Fuller's ideas about "rankism" changed my
personal behavior. I think they will change the world, in time.
It is one of those "click" realizations that you can't
unclick — everything human looks different afterward,
and you have to do something about it.

It's a book that parents should give their children, and a
must-read for anyone who cares about the future of this country.
Robert Fuller is sure to make the history books
with *Somebodies and Nobodies*.

The quest for recognition, especially by those who lack status,
has long been seen as one of the driving forces of human history.
Somebodies and Nobodies explains how recognition,
or its absence, affects your life, and what we can all
do to make sure that we treat each other with
the dignity we each deserve.

Somebody, nobody — in my time, I've been both. Most of us have.
Robert Fuller breaks the taboo on speaking about rank as others
have on race and gender. The message is simple; the message
is vital: protect the dignity of others as you do your own.
To be somebody, the nobody within you
has only to take a stand.

A wonderful call to action against the spillover of status.
Wealth, job title and social positions are too often
allowed to outweigh the respect to which each
human being is entitled.

— Roger Fisher, Director, Harvard Negotiation Project; author of *Getting to Yes*.

I've been treated like a nobody for too long.
I'm going to give a copy of this book to the principal
of my school on the day I leave.

— John F., 8th grade science teacher.

Absolutely life changing! After reading *Somebodies and Nobodies*,
I left the abusive job that I was in and searched for a
position that offered me the respect I deserved. Mr. Fuller's
book gave me the tools that I needed to know what
kind of supervisor I was looking for, and what kind
of questions to ask in interviews. Mr. Fuller is
a voice for those who feel that they do
not have the power to speak.

— Joanne Conger, development director for a nonprofit organization

Occasionally, an author comes along who makes us see
the world around us in a totally new way. Robert Fuller
takes us on a journey through the world of "ranks."
He explores how rank has been used throughout history to divide,
separate and control people. Equally important, he tells
us what we can do to overcome this outmoded and
destructive social mechanism and establish social relationships
based on the restoration and extension of the notion of
dignity. This book is an eye-opener that we can all
learn and benefit from in our daily lives.

— Jeremy Rifkin, President of the Foundation on Economic Trends in Washington,
D.C.; author of *The Age of Access and The Hydrogen Economy*.

At the core of every humiliation and indignity is a mental error, not just a habit — a lacuna so vast and unremitting that it passes unnoticed. You don't fix such a thing. It is not something to be patched. Nothing can be done until it is noticed, until it is named. Naming creates distinctions, distinctions create the capacity to change. Naming "rankism" transforms everything.

— Paul Hawken, author of *Natural Capitalism*.

This book is a must read for anyone who has wondered what the missing ingredient to a truly fair society is. The roadmap to a Dignitarian Society lies between the pages of *Somebodies and Nobodies*.

— Laura Adams, homemaker and mother of three

Robert Fuller refreshingly revives the case for serious mutual respect among all human beings, and indeed foresees the struggle for individual dignity, and an attack on its nemesis, "rankism," as the next great public movement in the United States. An insightful, thought-provoking, and novel treatment of an age-old subject.

— Richard N. Cooper, Maurits C. Boas Professor of International Economics, Harvard University; Undersecretary of State for Economic Affairs in the Carter administration.

In many ballet companies, young dancers are constantly being stripped of their humanity, innate sense of artistry, and individuality by the internal abuse of power. Just imagine how brilliantly dance would move forward without the weight of this oppression! Thanks to Robert Fuller for identifying the "rankism" that has been holding back our creativity for centuries.

— Brook Broughton, former professional dancer.

Simply brilliant. A rare treat full of insight, inspiration and plain, sane Common Sense. A modern-day Thomas Paine, Robert Fuller argues persuasively that democracy will only realize its full potential when "dignitarians" unite to overcome "rankism," the archetype of all "isms" — imperialism, colonialism, anti-Semitism, racism, sexism.

— Jeff Gates, author of *The Ownership Solution and Democracy at Risk*.

Somebodies and Nobodies will precipitate a national conversation about a pervasive but, until now, unnamed social dysfunction — "rankism." Watch for a "dignitarian" movement against rankism that, like the civil rights and women's movements, will transform American life — in the boardroom, the schoolroom, the bedroom and, a lot sooner than we might think, at the ballot box.

— Jerry Greenfield, co-founder of Ben and Jerry's Ice Cream.

We know from statistics that US society has become dramatically more unequal over the past generation. But Robert Fuller excavates the real-life stories behind the numbers, showing how "rankism" tramples on human dignity. *Somebodies and Nobodies* is a lucid and provocative manifesto for a more equal, and therefore more just, social order.

— Robert Pollin, co-author of *The Living Wage: Building a Fair Society*, Professor of Economics and Co-Director, Political Economy Research Institute, University of Massachusetts-Amherst.

Robert Fuller's insightful book has penetrated to the core of human dignity. He helps us understand why nearly all of us, even those with visible status and power, often feel belittled and diminished as human beings by the power of still higher status. But *Somebodies and Nobodies* is more than a diagnosis; it is a new way forward toward a society that takes seriously the deep conviction that we are truly all created equal.

— Peter Schwartz, Chairman, Global Business Network; author of *The Art of the Long View*.

Robert Fuller's book is a must-read for progressives of
every stripe. It enables us to resolve a confusing core issue central
to both society and our personal lives — hierarchy vs. equality.
For decades, our value of equality in relationships and desire
for "flatter" organizational structures has been challenged
by our daily experience of rank and hierarchy, such as
the natural hierarchy of parent-child, the organizational
ladder of boss-underling at work, or that of director,
staff, and volunteers in nonprofit groups. Robert Fuller
shows us how to distinguish between appropriate ranking
and the abuse of rank — "rankism" — and set aside the
latter in our personal relationships, our organizations,
and our international relations.

— Bill Moyer, author of *Doing Democracy*.

This book should be required reading for everyone in the
health care community where, sadly, "rankism" still thrives.
The "initiation" mentality, whereby old-timers who suffered rankist
abuse on their way up impose the same indignities on novices, is
still commonplace. I was unprepared to find myself in this book, but
I did. Reminded of past humiliations, I was outraged; catching
a glimpse of myself as a perpetrator, I was chagrined.

— Elizabeth Jones, medical services coordinator, surgical and hemodialysis technician.

Somebodies and Nobodies is important and original.
Fuller coins more than phrases; he coins concepts. You've heard of
attention deficit disorder. Think about the damage done by a
"recognition disorder." You've heard about egalitarian leveling
as a solution to inequality. Fuller gives us a "dignitarian" approach
to inevitable differences of power and status. The book's organizing
concept — "rankism" — links politics and ethics in a way that
provides new hope and direction to those seeking social justice.

— Jay Ogilvy, co-founder of Global Business Network;
former professor of philosophy at Yale University;
author of *Creating Better Futures* and *Living without a Goal*.

SOMEBODIES
AND NOBODIES

SOMEBODIES
AND NOBODIES

OVERCOMING *the* ABUSE OF RANK

ROBERT W. FULLER

NEW SOCIETY PUBLISHERS

Cataloguing in Publication Data:
A catalog record for this publication is available from the National Library of Canada.

Cover design by Diane McIntosh. Image: Artville RF (illustrator: Stephen F. Hayes).

Printed in Canada by Friesens.

ISBN: 0-86571-487-8

Inquiries regarding requests to reprint all or part of *Somebodies and Nobodies: Overcoming the Abuse of Rank* should be addressed to New Society Publishers at the address below.

To order directly from the publishers, please add $4.50 shipping to the price of the first copy, and $1.00 for each additional copy (plus GST in Canada). Send check or money order to:

New Society Publishers
P.O. Box 189, Gabriola Island, BC V0R 1X0, Canada
1-800-567-6772

New Society Publishers' mission is to publish books that contribute in fundamental ways to building an ecologically sustainable and just society, and to do so with the least possible impact on the environment, in a manner that models this vision. We are committed to doing this not just through education, but through action. We are acting on our commitment to the world's remaining ancient forests by phasing out our paper supply from ancient forests worldwide. This book is one step towards ending global deforestation and climate change. It is printed on acid-free paper that is **100% old growth forest-free** (100% post-consumer recycled), processed chlorine free, and printed with vegetable based, low VOC inks. For further information, or to browse our full list of books and purchase securely, visit our website at:

NEW SOCIETY PUBLISHERS   www.newsociety.com

To

Robert Moors Cabot

TABLE OF CONTENTS

Note to the Reader

Although I occasionally cite historical and philosophical works and include them among the related readings, this book is neither scholarly nor academic in the traditional sense. It is personal. The ideas in it have grown out of my experiences as a child, and later as the father of four; as a patient in the health care system; as an employee and employer; as a student, teacher, and college president; and as a world traveler and observer of international affairs.

These stages on life's way were punctuated by visits to "Nobodyland" (described herein), and it was during one such sojourn that new words to an old slogan began sounding in my head: "Nobodies of the world, unite; we have nothing to lose but our shame." At that point, I realized that the personal is political and began writing something I at first called "The Nobody Book."

In the spring of 2000, a version of this text was posted on a website devoted to rank and its abuse. Visitors to <breakingranks.net> provided many compelling examples of rank-based inequity. Almost everyone had a tale to tell of being "nobodied," and I've used some of their stories in these pages to help show how to recognize this kind of discrimination, and how to confront it.

The purpose of *Somebodies and Nobodies* is to break the taboo on the subject of rank, and reexamine the prerogatives that accompany status in relations between individuals, groups, and nations. Breaking taboos is always a risky business, and often causes discomfort. But it can also be liberating, and yield new strategies for solving intractable problems. Many of the difficulties we face in personal relationships, schools, and the workplace stem from the misuse of power associated with rank. So too with some of our most daunting national and international challenges — from the failures of education to economic exploitation to human rights violations and terrorism.

For many centuries in China, the worst form of torture was known as "death by a thousand cuts." What we have in the world today is "death by a thousand indignities," the stifling of the spirit of millions upon millions who are disenfranchised, dispossessed, or who, for whatever reason, experience themselves as living wasted lives. *Somebodies and Nobodies* is about the universal human desire for respect and participation, and the aberrant and dangerous behaviors that arise when this desire is thwarted.

The peace in our neighborhoods and around the globe is threatened by countless overt and covert abuses of rank, on scales both large and small. Given the lethality of weapons now available to aggrieved individuals and countries, it is essential we ensure that beyond basic needs, no one is deprived of the chance to contribute meaningfully to society, and to enjoy adequate recognition for those contributions. Accomplishing this will require overcoming the abuse of rank that sustains the present gap in dignity and opportunity between "somebodies" and "nobodies."

Chapter One

A DISORDER WITHOUT A NAME

The Personal is Political

As a student at Oberlin College during the 1950s, I was taught to be proud of its early advocacy of equal opportunity for women and blacks. But by the late 1960s, Oberlin students, like their counterparts across America, were in rebellion. The few dozen black students on campus were protesting their paltry numbers. Women students were criticizing the status of women in the college and the country. And many students who were upset over national policy on Vietnam turned their ire on whatever college policies impinged on their rights as young adults.

When Oberlin's Board of Trustees appointed me president of the college in 1970, the choice was clear: either embrace the changes "blowing in the wind" or be blown away. Within a few years, Oberlin, like most other colleges, added many African-Americans to its student body, faculty, and staff. Simultaneously, a feminist revolution transformed the College in a thousand subtle ways, and student pressure brought overdue reforms to social and educational policies.

The simultaneous activities of the black, women's, and student movements made me realize that there was something deeper going on. Something beyond differences in color, gender, and educational credentials underpinned the racism, sexism, and disenfranchisement of students that lay claim to our immediate attention. I sensed that the familiar "isms" were all manifestations of a more fundamental cause of discrimination, but I couldn't put my finger on it. It was not until I had left the presidency and had become a target of this kind of discrimination myself that I was able to identify it.

Lacking the protection of title and status in the years after Oberlin, I experienced what it's like to be taken for a "nobody." I found myself comparing the somebody-nobody divide with the white-black polarity of racism, the male-female opposition of sexism, and the teacher-student dichotomy in schools. There were differences, but there were similarities as well, the most important ones being (1) indignity and humiliation feel pretty much the same to a nobody, a black, a woman, or a student, and (2) no matter the excuse for abuse, it persists only in the presence of an underlying difference of rank signifying power. No one would dare to insult Queen Elizabeth I or General Colin Powell.

In the US, perhaps twenty percent of us have suffered directly from racism, and about fifty percent from sexism. But virtually all of us suffer from rank-based abuse — which I shall be calling "rankism" — in one context or another, at one time or another. Sooner or later, everyone gets taken for a nobody. Sooner or later, most of us treat someone else as a nobody. It always hurts to be "dissed," no matter what your status. Yet if it weren't for the fact that most everyone has known the sting of rankism, would there ever have been empathy for victims of racism and sexism?

At first I thought that rankism was just another ism, one more in the litany of isms with which we were growing weary, and I resisted the notion. Then it dawned on me that the familiar isms could be seen as subspecies of rankism. Racism, sexism, anti-Semitism, ageism and others all depend for their existence on differences of social rank that in turn reflect underlying power differences, so they are forms of rankism. Overcoming rankism would therefore undermine racism, sexism, and other isms that have been fought under those names but ultimately derive their force from power differences woven into the social fabric.

Gradually, I realized that the gains would go much further. For example, the reason so many students — regardless of color — withhold their hearts and minds from learning can be traced to the fact that their top priority and constant concern is to shield themselves from the rankism that permeates education from kindergarten to graduate school.

Rankism erodes the will to learn, distorts personal relationships, taxes economic productivity, and stokes ethnic hatred. It is the cause of dysfunctionality, and sometimes even violence, in families, schools, and the workplace. Like racism and sexism, rankism must be named and identified and then negotiated out of all our social institutions.

How could a scourge like rankism have gone thus far unremarked? Well, of course, it has not. We've been traumatized and battered by one or another of its manifestations for centuries, and many of these have long been recognized and acquired individual names. The situation is analogous to the era in medicine when malignancies peculiar to different organs were seen as disparate diseases. In time they were all recognized to be various forms of one disease — cancer.

Regardless of surface distinctions such as ethnicity, religion, color, or gender, persistent abuse and discrimination is predicated on power differences inherent in rank. Race-based discrimination is called racism, gender-based discrimination is called sexism. By analogy, rank-based discrimination can be called rankism.

Rankism is the "cancer" that underlies many of the seemingly disparate maladies that afflict the body politic. Unnamed, it will continue to debilitate, damage, and destroy; named, we can begin to unravel its pathology and take steps to protect ourselves. Attacking the familiar isms singly, one at a time, is like developing a different chemotherapy for each kind of cancer. To go after rankism directly is to seek to eliminate a whole class of malignancies.

Once you have a name for it, you see it everywhere. The outrage over self-serving corrupt executives is indignation over rankism. Sexual abuse by clergy is rankism. Elder abuse in life care facilities is rankism. Scientists taking credit for their assistants' research is rankism. More generally, rank-based discrimination is an ever-present reality in society at large, where it takes its greatest toll on those lacking the protections of social rank — the working poor. In her book *Nickel and Dimed: On (Not) Getting By in America*, Barbara Ehrenreich argues that the working poor are unacknowledged benefactors whose labor effectively subsidizes everyone else. The "living wage" movement is a harbinger of a "dignitarian" movement against social rankism.

The casualties of pell-mell globalization — economic and environmental — are attributable to rankism. International terrorism has complex origins and multiple causes, but one of them — and one within our control — is rankism, both inadvertent and intentional, between nations. There is no fury like that borne of chronic humiliation.

The effects of rankism on its targets are the same as those of racism and sexism on minorities and women. But unlike these familiar isms, rankism knows no limits and plays no favorites. It afflicts people of every race, gender, age, and class.

It is crucial to get one thing straight from the start: power differences, in themselves, are not the culprit. To bemoan power differences is like bemoaning the fact that the sun is brighter than the moon. And rank differences merely reflect power differences, so rank differences are not the problem either, any more than color or gender differences are innately a problem. Difficulties arise only when these differences are used as an excuse to abuse, humiliate, exploit, and subjugate. So it is with power and rank. Power differences are a fact of life. Making it okay to discuss the uses of power with those holding positions of authority, with an eye towards distinguishing between appropriate and inappropriate uses of their power, is what this book is about.

Typically, the abuse of the power vested in rank-holders takes the form of disrespect, inequity, discrimination, and exploitation. Since hierarchies are pyramids of power, rankism is a malady to which hierarchies of all types are susceptible.

Let's begin with a simple example of interpersonal rankism:

> An executive pulls up to valet parking at a restaurant, late to a business lunch, and finds no one to take his car keys. Anxious and fuming, he spots a teenager running toward him in the rear-view mirror and yells, "Where the hell were you? I haven't got all day."
>
> He tosses the keys at the kid's feet. Bending to pick them up, the boy says, "Sorry, sir. About how long do you expect to be?"
>
> The executive hollers over his shoulder, "You'll know when you see me, won't you?" The valet winces, but holds his tongue. Postscript: he goes home and bullies his kid brother.

Further examples leap to mind: a boss harassing an employee, a cook or a customer demeaning a server, a coach bullying a player, a doctor disparaging a nurse, a school principal insulting a teacher, a professor exploiting a teaching assistant, a teacher humiliating a student, students ostracizing other students, a parent belittling a child, an officer abusing a suspect, a caretaker mistreating an invalid.

Again, it's not that rank itself is illegitimate. When rank has been earned and signifies excellence, then it's generally accepted, and rightfully so. But the power of rank can be and often is abused, as in the examples above. Power begets power, authority becomes entrenched, and rank-holders become self-aggrandizing, capricious, and overbearing. Most of us have tasted rankism; for many, it's a dietary staple.

Rankism insults the dignity of subordinates by treating them as invisible, as nobodies. Nobody is another n-word and, like the original, it is used to justify denigration and inequity. Nobodies are insulted, disrespected, exploited, ignored. In contrast, somebodies are sought after, given preference, lionized.

You may be thinking that rankism is just a new name for bullying. While bullying is indeed archetypal rankism, the old word has limited range. The term rankism is more inclusive, grouping disparate actions by their common underlying cause and affording us a fresh look at behaviors we now put up with, sometimes collude in and, on occasion, indulge in ourselves.

Rankism — Mother of "Isms"

It might be supposed that if one overcame tendencies to racism, sexism, ageism and other narrowly defined forms of discrimination, one would be purged of rankism as well. But rankism is not just another ism. It subsumes the familiar dishonorable isms. It's the mother of them all.

What makes it possible for one group to discriminate against another? For example, whites segregating blacks, Gentiles imposing quotas on Jews, or straights harassing gays? Color, religion, gender, and sexual orientation are simply pretexts for constructing and exploiting social stratifications; they are not the actual cause of ongoing injustice. Such discrimination is predicated on social dominance that depends on established, constructed power differences, fortified by customs and laws. As the power gap closes through the breakdown of customs and the repeal of prejudicial legislation, systemic abuse becomes harder and harder to sustain.

Like other predators, human beings select as prey those they perceive as weak. It's a safer bet; there's less chance of retaliation. Distinguishing traits such as color, gender, or sexual orientation only signify weakness if there is a social consensus in place that handicaps those bearing the trait. A social consensus such as Jim Crow, the feminine mystique, or homophobia functions to keep an entire group of people weak and usable by the dominant group (whites, males, or straights, in these cases).

Power matters. In fact, it's more or less all that matters, and it is important for those who temporarily lack it to realize this so they can set about building a countervailing power. It is only as those subordinated by a particular consensus organize and gain power commensurate with that of their oppressors that the prevailing consensus unravels and the pretext for exploitation is disallowed.

Although rank-based discrimination *feels* the same to its targets as the more familiar kinds, there are some important differences in the way it works. Unlike race or gender, rank is mutable. You can be taken for a nobody one day and for a somebody the next. You can be a nobody at home and a somebody at work, or vice versa. The mutability of rank means that most of us have been both victims and perpetrators of rankism, in different contexts.

Rankism, like racism, is a source of social injustice as well as personal indignity. As we'll see, a great deal of what's labeled social pathology has its origins in rankism. But unlike racists and sexists, who are now on notice, rankists still go largely unchallenged. The indignity suffered by those who've been "nobodied" festers. It builds to indignation and sometimes erupts in violence. When a person or a people is nobodied, it not only does them an injustice, but also plants a time bomb in our midst.

The consequences range from school shootings to revanchism, even to genocide. The twentieth century has seen many demagogues who have promised to restore the pride and dignity of a people that felt nobodied. Hitler enjoyed the support of Germans humiliated by punitive reparations in the aftermath of World War I. The national impotence imposed on the German nation (the Fatherland) by the victors reverberated through every German family, as well. In opting for Hitler, many Germans were not only voting to restore rank to the Fatherland, but also to overcome the sense of inadequacy they'd experienced as the heads of German families. Similarly, President Milosevic of Yugoslavia traded on the wounded pride of the Serbs in the 1990s. Once war begins, people will become apologists for crimes they would otherwise condemn to get even with those they believe have nobodied them.

Globally, there are few counterparts to the democratic institutions that mitigate the most flagrant displays of rankism within nations. However, nowhere are rankism's effects more acute than in the still largely extra-legal realm of international relations; weaker states are often compelled to do the bidding of stronger ones.

In the distinction between rank and rankism lies the difference between dignity and indignity — for persons, for peoples, for nations. A truly great power, to be worthy of the name, distinguishes itself from a "mere" superpower through its sensitivity to this difference in its dealings with weaker states.

Attacking the familiar isms, one at a time, is like lopping heads off the Hydra of discrimination and oppression; going after rankism aims to drive a stake through the Hydra's heart.

Equal in Dignity

Dignity is not negotiable.
> —Vartan Gregorian, American writer, university president, and foundation
> executive (1934 –   )

Though most of us have experienced rankism, we do not routinely protest it, at least not to the perpetrators. We limit our complaints to those who share our station. Uncle Tom's policy of "to get along, go along" recommends itself to almost everyone when it comes to confronting rankism. As a short-term solution this is understandable because the power difference upon which rankism is predicated makes resisting it dangerous. But in the long run, appeasement fails. Uncle Tom ended up being whipped to death.

Despite the fact that we may acquiesce to unequal treatment or even collude in self-abnegation, most of us sense that there is something about human beings that is universal, absolute, and, yes, equal.

Equal? We are obviously unequal in skill, talent, beauty, strength, health, or wealth — in any measurable trait for that matter.

What then? For millennia, there have been people of every faith, often in opposition to their own religious leaders, who have sensed that all human beings are of equal *dignity*. Though this spiritual insight is routinely violated, it is grounded in (and represents an intuitive grasp of) more pragmatic reasons for opposing rankist abuses of power, reasons that we'll explore in the chapters to follow.

Rankism is invariably an assault on dignity. If people are fundamentally equal in dignity, then discrimination on the basis of power differences — experienced as an insult to dignity — has no legitimacy and must be disallowed. The notion of rankism links ethics and politics through dignity.

All ranks, like all races, are worthy of equal dignity. Deviations from equal dignity set in motion a dynamic that draws attention away from whatever we're doing — working, learning, or healing. When energy is diverted to defending one's dignity against insults in the workplace, productivity suffers. In schools, students sacrifice their learning to defend their dignity. Today, it is not so much racial prejudice as misuse of rank that functions to keep students of all colors from committing themselves to education. It is rankism that creates the specious divide between winners and losers at an early age and extinguishes ambition in many before they reach third grade.

More than other peoples, Americans seem to believe that if you fail, it's your own fault. Yet we all know of many instances where power, position, and privilege — not merit — have predetermined an outcome. The rich, the powerful, and the famous enjoy unearned perks in all walks of life. Celebrities go to the head of the line; their transgressions are forgiven. We hope to be treated evenhandedly, but are not surprised when we're not.

Over the centuries, the democratization of our civic institutions has curtailed the most blatant kinds of governmental rankism. But rising voter apathy now signals that the issues that matter most — education, health policy, and working conditions — are perceived as lying beyond the effective reach of government. The challenge is to find a way to bring the core principle of democracy — the idea of mutual accountability and non-rankist service — to all our social institutions.

The Myth of Meritocracy

America sees itself as a meritocracy, in contrast to aristocratic Europe. But while opportunity is more equal here than it was in aristocracies, it is still far from merit-based. The last half-century has seen an assault on race, gender, sexual orientation, and age-based barriers to equal opportunity, but the surface upon which we compete for recognition is still a steep hill, not a level playing field.

Paradoxically, it is rank itself that now poses the greatest obstacle to basing rewards on merit. This is because rank acquired in one realm often confers advantages in other, unrelated ones. Why should rank shield perpetrators from the consequences of rule-breaking, misdeeds, or incompetence? Why should it be harder for those of low rank to improve their station than for those of high rank to retain theirs? If rank is based on merit, high rank today should not be a guarantor of high rank tomorrow. Nor should low rank carry the stigma of perpetual loser. Discrimination based on rank differences is as inconsistent with actual meritocracy as is discrimination based on color or gender differences.

In a true meritocracy, rank would have to be precisely defined, and rewards would reflect current rank within a large and growing number of narrowly defined niches. High rank in one specialty, as determined on one occasion, would not signify merit in general or indefinitely. Because individuals' talents, abilities, and skills vary markedly from niche to niche, composite, overall rankings that ignore variations from specialty to specialty yield spurious results. We don't simply declare the winner of the mile the best runner, because that would overlook the fact that there are sprinters and marathoners who, in their events, can outdo the fastest miler. Merit has no significance, and therefore should carry no weight, beyond the precise realm wherein it is assessed. From this perspective, IQ measures not the broad amorphous trait "intelligence" — now recognized to assume a myriad of specialized forms — but rather the ability to do well on a particular kind of test. Similarly, ranking schools by their students' average test scores is a measure of how a selected group of students did on a particular test, not the schools' intrinsic educational merit.

Achievers of high rank often use their position to disadvantage those who would challenge them, or to hang on to rewards they may once have earned but since ceased to merit. An aura of social rank — a vestige of aristocratic class — envelops winners (who are seen as somebodies), and is denied to runners-up (who are seen as nobodies). Parents pay premiums to elite universities in the belief that the prestige of these famous schools will rub off on their offspring and bring them advantages after graduation.

Although most new organizations start out with the intention of doing good and providing a service, once rankism gains a foothold, like a parasitical disease, it subverts that purpose to the narrower goal of advancing the well-being of high-ranking members. The discriminatory, morale-sapping effects of rankism can be seen in hierarchies of all kinds: schools and universities; firms, corporations, and businesses; labor unions; medical, religious and nonprofit organizations; the guardian professions and the military; bureaucracies and governments.

Meritocracy is a myth in the presence of rankism, just as it was in the presence of racism and sexism. Until there are effective procedures that curtail rank-based discrimination in all of our social institutions, American meritocracy is unworthy of the name.

Democracy's Next Step

During the two centuries since the American and French Revolutions, and despite woeful lapses and delays, the franchise in modern democracies has gradually widened to include virtually all adults.

But although we've made significant inroads against racism and sexism, diminishing returns seem to be setting in. At this stage an all-inclusive approach might do more to advance the causes of minorities, women, and other identity groups than the splintering, sometimes divisive, group-based politics of recent years. A practical way to further justice at this point, including the rights of specific groups, is to attack the universal underlying cause of indignity, regardless of who is targeted. That cause is rankism.

Unequal opportunity and unfairness are incompatible with democratic ideals. The indignities of rankism, no less than those of racism and sexism, are inefficient, cruel, and self-defeating. They have no place in democracy's future.

In the 1960s, America faced a moral crisis that threatened to tear the country apart. Once we understood that there was no way to end the crisis without dismantling racism, we took steps to do so. As we enter the twenty-first century, a moral crisis looms that could become equally grave. Our political and economic institutions, both national international, are rife with rankism.

Democracy is a work in progress. Its essence is its capacity for self-correction. Overcoming rankism — in the family, the schools, the workplace, and the boardroom, and in domestic and international politics — is now at the top of democracy's agenda. The purpose of this book is to shine a spotlight on rank-based abuse, to learn to recognize its various faces, assess its costs, and conceive a world without it.

Like racism and sexism, rankism can't be eradicated overnight, but its perpetrators can be put on notice. Authority can be democratized without being undermined. Democracies, which succeeded in circumscribing rank in national government, led the world in the last century. The nations that are most successful in removing rankism from business, education, and their international relations will lead in the next.

Chapter Two

USES AND ABUSES OF RANK

Why Rank Matters

Rank is generally less conspicuous than race or gender, but every bit as consequential. No sooner do people meet, than they begin probing to determine each other's rank.

"What do you do?" Who hasn't been asked the soft question with the hard edge? Depending on our answer, our interrogator may treat us with deference or disregard. Rank entitles, and it limits. It's a source of pride, and of shame. We struggle for rank, and if we get it, we hang on. People will die in defense of their rank.

Tribal and national groups also covet rank. Over the course of history a succession of peoples — for example, the Romans, the French, the British, and the Americans — have prided themselves on being "Number One."

In everyday life, rank indicates position in a hierarchy, and it is expressed in a title. Our title signals our authority. It is as a signifier of power that rank acquires the extraordinary importance we attach to it.

When we think of rank, we may think first of the military, but rank is no less important in other hierarchies. In the traditional family, children are outranked by parents, and in some cultures the first-born outranks siblings. In the trades, we begin as an apprentice, rise to journeyman, and strive to become a master craftsman. In the firm, there are secretaries, bosses at every level, vice-presidents, and a chief executive officer. In academia, students are taught by instructors, assistant professors, associate professors, and, at the top of the academic ladder, "full" professors. Presiding over the faculty are the deans, provosts, vice-presidents, and a president. In medicine, patients are ministered to by health care providers whose ranks include patient care technicians, licensed practical nurses, registered nurses, interns, residents, and doctors.

Ranks are further subdivided with qualifiers such as "administrative," "associate," "senior," "managing," or "executive," or by adding suffixes such as "at Large" or "in Chief." Titles, and the ranks they distinguish, are important to us because they tell us who rules and who is expected to submit to whom.

Quite apart from our rank in the workplace, there is a more nebulous social rank — often referred to as "class" — that clings to us and defines our status in society at large. Social rank is inferred from attributes like connections, clothes, school ties, looks, talent, and wealth. Usually, high social rank carries advantages and low social rank functions as a handicap. In aristocratic societies, like Edwardian Britain, class was everything.

In the past, certain traits were tantamount to low, or at least dubious, social rank — traits like color, national origin, religion, wealth, and pedigree. Other characteristics such as gender, age, sexual orientation, and disability have also made their carriers vulnerable to abuse and discrimination. One by one, these have all been eliminated as justification for discrimination. The only criterion that still sanctions abuse and discrimination is rank itself.

The reason that rankism has outlasted these familiar forms of abuse and discrimination is that rank, when it has been earned, is a measure of excellence, and distinguishing degrees of excellence is vital to the success of any human enterprise. Thus, rank itself is not inherently illegitimate as a carrier of power. Organizing ourselves to work cooperatively has always depended on ranking people and giving some authority over others.

The problem isn't that rank counts. When it signifies excellence, rank should count and it does. The trouble is that rank counts twice. No sooner is rank assigned than holders of higher rank can use their newfound power to aggrandize themselves at the expense of those of lower ranks. Although some exercise their rank properly — within their area of competence and in a way that respects the dignity of those under their authority — others do not.

A social worker provides an example:

> I was a "senior citizen outreach worker" at the local YMCA. One of my co-workers was promoted to supervisor over the rest of the staff. Once in a position of authority, she became a tyrant. She ordered us around, took long lunch hours, created rules that made no sense and ill-served the elderly population with whom we worked.
>
> This woman was an African-American and I suspected that she was using her position to settle old scores, at last thumbing her nose at whites at whose hands she had suffered from racism. This Midwest city had a long history of tension between Appalachian whites and Southern blacks. For me the problem was how not to take her anger personally and at the same time hold her accountable for treating us with respect.

Legitimate Uses of Rank

Our status or rank signifies our relative place within a group. Like chickens in a pecking order, we outrank some and are outranked by others. But unlike a chicken coop, modern human societies comprise thousands of different hierarchies, and a person at the bottom of one may be at the top of another. The worst bowler on the company team may be the CEO; the college dropout may be a billionaire.

Rank is an essential tool in the management of our lives and our institutions. Comparison and judgment are necessary to select a computer or a car, admit or reject applicants to college, accept or decline an offer of marriage. Without ranking candidates by counting votes, how would we select people for political office?

Greater efficiency and productivity follow when we get the right person into the right job. To remain successful, an organization must appraise personnel continuously and accurately. Selectivity is predicated on ranking; without it, choice would simply be random. Within each niche where it has been earned, rank has proven utility, legitimacy, and deserves our respect.

People who hold rank often find themselves in the role of gatekeeper to those seeking it. I found myself in such a role while teaching physics at Columbia University. I received a manuscript from a local laundry man claiming that Einstein's theories were wrong and offering in their place his own theory which, he claimed, unified all the laws of physics. Realizing that this fellow's dreams were not different from my own, I felt duty bound to figure out if he'd made good on his claim. Hours later, having detected a few mistakes and feeling frustrated with his unconventional notation, I gave up and returned the manuscript with a polite but noncommittal note.

In the years that followed I received many such amateur offerings, as did my colleagues who typically dismissed their authors as "cranks." Before long I too was returning these submissions unread. The time and effort it would have taken to evaluate them fairly would have prevented me from reading my colleagues' papers and pursuing my own research. So I ended by rejecting them all. It's not egalitarian, but it's necessary. Science is not egalitarian. Neither is any art or craft. Judgment, discrimination, and ranking go to the heart of any human endeavor that aims at excellence. Ranking plays an essential role in time management, in selecting from all the people clamoring for our attention the few who are most likely to have something of pertinent value.

The awkward balancing act of the gatekeeper's job is implicit in the two opposed meanings of the word "discriminate." On the one hand, "discriminate" means to perceive the distinguishing features of, to discern, to select with intent. This is the proper job of someone responsible for quality control. On the other hand, "discriminate" means to distinguish categorically, on the basis of membership in a group, without regard for individual merit. Such discrimination is preferential or prejudicial. The former usage applies mainly to ideas and inanimate objects such as works of art, wines, and food, where it signals connoisseurship. To discriminate in this sense is necessary and good — it enriches our lives. The latter usage is typically applied to people where it means unfair exclusion or unjust treatment. The two meanings of "discriminate" lie at the heart of the difference between proper and improper uses of rank.

Not a few well-meaning utopians have sought to reduce the suffering of those who lose out in contests for rank by proposing rules that blur distinctions and promote more equal outcomes. But even if it were desirable, equality of outcomes seems unattainable. Human beings are too individual and too varied. The idealistic impulse to abolish rank and ranking is futile because people are unequal in their realized talents and abilities. This inequality has been evident since the first time two humans raced on the plains of Africa: one won, the other lost. Pity the loser, except that he probably went off and invented the spear.

In those times the rankings that mattered most were who was number one at fighting, running, and hunting. Dominance in these skills meant survival, and top ranking made you a tribal chief or king.

Today, thankfully, survival is no longer our constant concern and power is no longer synonymous with physical prowess. Contemporary adult life is replete with thousands of specialties, in all of which we may gain expertise and seek recognition. We give the fastest runner in each of a dozen different events a gold medal, and the best javelin thrower another, but none do we crown king. Today, we variously exercise a broad range of highly specialized skills in multiple ongoing contests civilized by laws and regulations, custom and manners. The struggle for rank has become less a matter of survival than of working our way up in the world. Although physical combat has given way to climbing the ladder of success, the goal remains the same — achieving rank, as gauged by status, title, office size, earnings, and so on.

Striving for high rank is more than a way of ascertaining competence and distributing power. It can be a source of deep gratification and joy. Earned rank brings with it the satisfaction of being recognized and appreciated for our talents, skills, and hard work. We value excellence in others because by emulating them we can make their winning ways our own.

Pulling Rank

Although there are situations in which rank is legitimately and necessarily "pulled" — a mother yanks her child out of the path of an oncoming bus — rank is so often abused that the phrase "pulling rank" has become synonymous, in common usage, with doing so unnecessarily and abusively.

Most of us have suffered in one way or another at the hands of people who outrank us. In fact, the high-ranking have such a consistent history of misusing the power of their position that today anyone assuming authority comes immediately under suspicion, especially from the young.

This example is from a restaurant server:

> I have worked in many restaurants and could tell you endless stories about psycho chefs throwing plates at my head, managers eating elaborate meals served by waitresses, and back-of-the-house staff who were given nothing to eat during the course of a ten-hour shift and were reduced to stealing scraps from the raw bar.
>
> The humiliation of having to dress up in yellow, black, and white milkmaid costumes was the least of it. More trying was dealing with the lascivious bartender who came on to me any time I had to order a "screwdriver."
>
> The cooks were all-powerful. They could mess up or slow down your order if they didn't like you, causing you to receive low or no tips. You didn't dare complain to the manager because a waitress is more expendable than a cook.

The problem is not hierarchy, but the abuse of rank within it. If cooks and servers in this establishment divided neatly along traditional gender lines, waitresses might eventually get together and accuse the cooks of sexism. But since many establishments now employ both male and female cooks and servers, it's clear that problems of this kind involve the abuse of rank.

When rank is won because the rules or the judges favor some contestants at the expense of others, resentment builds. If unfairness persists, losers may become smoldering volcanoes, dreaming of vengeance and sometimes exacting it when they get the opportunity. School misfits turn on their classmates. "Nerds," ridiculed and cast out as youths, grow up to sow computer viruses. Humiliated groups or peoples are more likely to support terrorists.

Three Vignettes

A contractor recalling his days as an apprentice carpenter:

> Most of the contractors I worked for during my apprenticeship were "screamers." If you asked for help, they'd yell, "You should know that by now." If you made a mistake it was the end of the world.
>
> There are contractors who just put you on foundations. You never get a chance to do the framing or the trim work; you're just a grunt. How can you learn the trade like that? And when they're through with you they send you down the road.
>
> The worst is working for a contractor who has his son working, or a cousin, nephew, or friend. As someone without connections, you get the digging, the form stripping, the concrete pouring. You're also expected to have a good attitude. Only the boss's relatives are allowed to bitch. You feel that you're judged on a whim and not on what you produce.
>
> One contractor told me, "All I want to see are your elbows and your ass." He wanted me bent over, working at all times. Even lunch was a walking sandwich. The ultimate humiliation is when contractors don't provide temporary toilet facilities, so you have to relieve yourself in the bushes.

A 7th grade science teacher:

> Everyone assumes they know everything about teaching and that it's easy. When I'm out with my wife's lawyer friends, it's always clear that they assume a superior professional position. Law and finance are hyper-important, while education is seen as commonplace and beneath them.

Lawyers assume they hold high rank because of their incomes and financial power — that because teachers get paid less, they have lower rank. Also, teachers work with kids, which lowers them even further. We're the lowest rung on the professional ladder.

A top executive of a leading pharmaceutical company, having achieved personal financial security at 45, quits to try something new:

I had a succession of ever more impressive business cards during my career. On my way up the ladder, they defined me — title and company. The response was always very positive.

When I retired I printed up new business cards with only my name, address, and phone number. The response to this name-only ID was that I had become a nobody. Without title and institutional affiliation, people didn't know how to calibrate my value. They no longer saw me as having anything to offer, and for several years, I'm sorry to say, I believed this myself.

These three individuals are all white males. They run the gamut from blue-collar to independently wealthy. Clearly, their distress cannot be chalked up to race or gender or class. What they have in common is that they have felt discounted and invisible. Each of them feels his dignity has been insulted. Each feels nobodied.

Of course we all have to put up with evaluation and criticism to get where we want in life. But have you ever wondered why we're so quick to see others, and sometimes even ourselves, as nobodies, as losers? Or why those who've made it to the top — the somebodies — feel that gives them the right to lord it over those who have not?

In struggles to gain recognition, rules of fairness are sometimes overlooked. Cheat your competitors if you can get away with it. Play dirty, just don't get caught. If you win, denigrate the losers. If you lose, disparage the winners.

Insults to dignity leave wounds on the psyche just as stones do on the body. Over a lifetime, these insults add up. They rankle. We remember them, and they affect us in ways that are awkward to discuss. Who wants to admit they *ever* felt like a nobody? We all want to be treated with respect — today, tomorrow, until our dying breath. And if you've never been nobodied and believe you never will be, you haven't paid a visit to a nursing home.

Kicking the Dog

Objects of bullying seldom just absorb insult and transmute it into beneficence. "Turning the other cheek" is high-minded, risky, and rare. Although the power difference deters targets from retaliating directly against an oppressor, they *can* take their rage out on someone they perceive as weaker than themselves. The relativity of rank means that although everybody is a nobody to someone, everybody is also a somebody to someone else. Humiliated in one context, we may assert ourselves over someone who is less powerful than we are. It's not surprising that kids who witness their elders picking on the weak mirror this bullying behavior. Here's a teacher reminiscing about herself as a seventh grader:

> I was in the out group. I was a sweet, sensitive girl who followed all the rules, but I was ugly. Frizzy hair. Big nose. Bad skin. Often I'd come home in tears because of the teasing from my classmates.
>
> I remember there was a school talent show. Tim, a fellow outcast, somehow gathered the courage to sing "The House of the Rising Sun." He'd probably imagined this moment over and over — it was his chance to be somebody. Well, as soon as he got up on stage and started singing, the catcalls started. He could barely finish his song.
>
> You'd think that after being the target of similar abuse I might have stood up for him, or at least stayed quiet. But instead, I joined in the jeering. "Yeah, that Tim is such a jerk." I felt so relieved that for once the target wasn't me.

Until we can see how to organize against an abuse of power, we acquiesce, sometimes letting off steam by attacking those we outrank: I'll put up with the cruel indignities you throw my way, so long as I can dish them out to my subordinates. At the top of the status ladder are society's lions; at the very bottom are nobodies' nobodies. And what do *they* do, the people at the very bottom? They kick the dog.

As part of a science lab, students in a course I taught for high school dropouts were given live frogs to etherize for dissection. One of the boys horrified the class by announcing that he was going to skin his frog alive. He was fat and awkward and the object of social cruelty. This was his chance to get even — on a defenseless frog — and to send his classmates a message about just how tough and ruthless he could be.

The entertainment value of humiliation, a staple of television and movies, derives from this same source. The perverse pleasure of witnessing the denigration of some hapless victim on the screen is a way of letting go of our internalized, pent-up rage. Nothing, however, is more enjoyable than seeing a target of rankism *get even* with his or her tormentors.

Very few people are impervious to having rank pulled on them, and fewer still are entirely innocent of doing it themselves. Even those who ordinarily treat others with equal respect may be provoked into responding in kind if they are patronized, or their dignity is insulted. Reactive rankism is something I've seen in myself. For a long time, I thought it was justified. Then I noticed that I was retaliating reflexively, with scarcely a pause between the incoming insult and the one returned in kind. For a while I continued to rationalize that I'd not gone first, I'd not initiated the offense, but over the years that argument has become hollow.

With regard to insults to dignity, everyone is "going second." Everyone is still smarting from some slight or other, and is waiting for a chance to retaliate by passing it off onto someone else, even an innocent bystander. It is especially important for those who have surmounted indignities and finally "made it" to be careful they do not force others to pay the price for the pain they suffered on the way up. Under no circumstances does status excuse rankist behavior.

Often, people who act belligerently do so out of an unconscious fear that others are trying to dominate them. Once they are reassured on this count, they become friendly and cooperative, showing no need themselves to dominate. Allaying these fears in each other is part of self-defense.

Domestic abuse, bigotry, and "hate crimes" are all fueled by the rankist impulse to kick the dog. Wife-beaters, gay-bashers, and lynch mobs can all be seen as displacing disdain they have themselves experienced on to the undefended.

Is Pulling Rank Human Nature?

Many people believe that it's human nature to pull rank and that nothing can be done about it. But the turnabout of attitudes toward racism and sexism that we've witnessed in the last half-century suggests that opposing rank-based abuse and discrimination is not hopeless. Once parents stop, kids follow suit. As the lyrics in *South Pacific* say, "You've got to be taught to hate."

Furthermore, despite easy talk to the contrary, the powerful do not always do as they please. In countries under the rule of law, the rich and powerful observe the property and other constitutional rights of those weaker than themselves. The rule of law is nothing if it does not apply equally to all. There is no reason to believe that the privileged cannot be brought to view rankism in the same way that most of us have now come to view racism and sexism — as behaviors no longer to be sanctioned. It is not hard to imagine a day when everyone's right to equal dignity will be as self-evident as everyone's right to own property or to free speech.

As new technologies are developed that afford their owners temporary advantages, abuses of power will undoubtedly continue to appear in human affairs. But if anything is human nature, it is the will to democracy — that is, the will to curtail abuses of rank by acting together to create systems of governance that circumscribe authority. History shows that democracy is not weaker than the tyrannies it supplants, or those that would challenge it from without. On the contrary, whenever the citizens of a democracy have closed ranks in its defense, they've repeatedly proven capable of generating a surpassing strength.

The first step is, of course, to make people aware of rank as an excuse for abuse. As we become adept at distinguishing between rank's legitimate and illegitimate applications, collective opposition to its abuses becomes possible, instance by instance.

During the period before we confront a specific abuse of power, we tend to see the affronts we suffer as facts of life. Indeed, until we have organized a counterforce, rankism cannot even be defined except in the imaginations of those with the moral prescience to sense that human dignity is somehow being transgressed. I shall return to the transcendental nature of rankism later on; but first I'll address some familiar kinds of rank-based discrimination with the goal of showing that rankism, once it is recognized as such, is no more invincible than were racism and sexism.

Chapter Three

THE TOLL OF RANK ABUSE

The abuse of rank typically involves using the power associated with it to improve or secure one's lot to the disadvantage of others. This can take the form of feathering one's nest, making one's position impregnable, or erecting barriers that impose disadvantages on would-be challengers. Rank in one realm is parlayed into dominance in another. So long as people use rank acquired in one setting to secure power for themselves in another, contests for recognition will be unfair.

Let's look now at some specific areas of our lives and the toll that rankism takes on each of them.

On Personal Relationships

The abuse of rank is experienced by victims as an insult to their dignity. Our antennae are tuned to detect the slightest trace of condescension or disrespect in others' treatment of us; we speak of someone looking down his or her nose at us. A woman in her late forties writes:

> Upon graduating from college I took a job in food service at a local university teaching hospital to earn money for graduate studies in music. My job — delivering trays to patients while wearing a polyester uniform and hair net — was certainly not a glamorous one. Often, as I wielded my cumbersome cart through

the halls, I was blocked by clusters of medical interns on their rounds. They exuded self-importance and ignored me and I was forced to maneuver ever so carefully around them. After a while, in anger and frustration, I would deliberately run over toes. One day I stepped into an elevator in which there were two handsome young male interns. One looked at me, smiled and gave me a shy, friendly "Hi." I returned the smile and hello. His buddy, eyeing the exchange, nudged him and said to him in a low snicker, "Slumming in the elevator?" That was 25 years ago and I still remember it. To this day I regret not having had the presence of mind to object to his behavior.

In personal relations, pulling rank takes the form of disrespect, disregard, disdain, "dissing," berating, snobbism, insult and humiliation. But as with racism, what may seem abusive on the face of it is not necessarily so. I was shocked when I first heard African-Americans using the n-word to each other. But it soon became clear that these apparent insults were actually disguised declarations of affection among peers. Humorous intent can also shift the meaning of a word or phrase that, taken literally, would be an affront, to an expression of endearment. Trading insults can be a game — trash-talking — that transforms what would otherwise be incivility into playful verbal jousting. Irony can redeem the apparently irredeemable.

Generally, however, interpersonal abuse in the context of a difference of rank is antithetical to reciprocity, mutuality, and equality. It is meant to demean, to exploit, to wound, to harm, and to damage — and it does. No wonder that under assault we are wary and withdrawn, not open-minded and generous. Even when not deliberately malicious, rank abuse can still warp our interactions.

The following example from a female Ph.D. student suggests the part that sexual desirability plays in determining women's social rank:

> I am bisexual. When I started my doctoral program I was in a relationship with a woman. The head of the department was heterosexual and liked to flirt with women students. I found myself uncharacteristically hiding the fact that I was involved with a woman, sensing that if he knew, my power to flirt would

be reduced and with it my influence within our departmental governance system. He had strong opinions, and offered teaching assistantships and other perks to people whom he favored. He was a complicated man: I respected his mind and his commitment to international development, but he did favor attractive, flirtatious women and that gave them advantages. I still feel ashamed that I was not more forthcoming about my relationship (after all, I loved my partner), but I feared subtle but harmful consequences.

The first step toward making rank-based abuse unacceptable is to learn to spot it wherever it appears. For example, sexual harassment, wherein a boss seeks to gain sexual favors from a subordinate, is a classic example of pulling rank. If the boss required a financial payoff from an underling in exchange for preference in the workplace, we would call it extortion. By analogy, if someone of higher rank demands a sexual payoff in exchange for preferment on the job, we should call it the same thing: extortion — an abuse of power.

The 1998 court-martial of Sergeant Major Gene McKinney, the Army's highest-ranking enlisted man, on charges of sexual misconduct illuminates the relative nature of rank and demonstrates that the same person can simultaneously be both a perpetrator and a target of rank abuse. When McKinney was charged with sexually harassing his female subordinates, he counter-claimed that his superiors were discriminating against *him* on the basis of *his* rank. His attorneys contended that had McKinney been a commissioned officer — a member of "the general's club" — the Army would have cut him a deal and let him retire without facing charges. There have been numerous cases, before and since McKinney's, in which this is precisely what happened. The military court found in McKinney's favor.

An example of sexual harassment reported by a therapist starkly reveals its link to rank:

> The dean of a law school would hit on the lower paid workers, groping them, but would flirt only verbally with the high-ranked staff (e.g., the registrar). The liberties he took were a function of women's rank and position. The ones who didn't

get paid much got fondled; the more highly paid got cozied up to but were spared any real humiliation.

Not holding the powerful to the same legal standards as everyone else has no doubt been going on since early strongmen showed favoritism to their relatives. Nowadays it often takes the form of money buying justice. Leaving aside outright bribery, the rich can afford a "dream team" of defense lawyers and jury consultants; the poor must make do with court-appointed public defenders. Corporations hire phalanxes of attorneys, complemented by highly paid expert witnesses. Justice, which is based on the adversarial system, cannot be evenhanded if the adversaries have unequal resources or competence.

Politics is a realm in which centuries of struggle have resulted in certain kinds of rank abuse losing their sanction. The democratic ideal is that the state serves the people, not the other way round, and to the extent that this ideal of service is realized, rank abuse is held in check. But in practice, politics still runs on campaign contributions that incline legislators to betray the public trust by serving not those who voted for them, but rather the special interests that paid for their television commercials. The buying of representatives' votes by special interests and corporations guts the democratic ideal and, unchecked, leads to government by the wealthy — plutocracy.

Another locus of rank-pulling, long taken for granted, is the traditional doctor-patient relationship. Until recently, no one dared question "the doctor's orders." Physicians sent their adult patients to bed like children, and people made vulnerable by illness acquiesced in their own infantilization. Today the relationship between doctor and patient is in turmoil and flux. As the writer Anna Quindlen says, "The day of the MDeity should be over; doctors have acted like little gods because patients have treated them as though they were." Faced with more choices and emboldened by knowledge gleaned from books, support groups, and the Internet, people are transforming themselves from compliant patients into informed customers. Doctors can no longer hold themselves aloof from probing questions. Partnerships between medical professionals and their clients are replacing traditional doctor-patient relationships as more people become actively involved in their own health care and relate to doctors as professional consultants.

In its milder forms, the power of rank to distort relationships reveals itself in the many ways we flatter those who we believe outrank us and demean or ignore those below us in the pecking order. We learn the names of our doctors, but not those of their assistants who schedule our appointments and phone in our prescriptions. We're outraged if a client refuses to pay for our services, yet we may skimp on tips. We expect our employer to pay our benefits and contribute to our social security, yet we do not provide the same to those who do household labor for us. The point of citing these examples is not to accuse, but rather to heighten awareness of the ways in which we may deviate from the principle and the practice of equal dignity for all.

Like racism, rank abuse has an institutional face as well as an interpersonal one. When the power inherent in a position of authority is used to fortify that position, the institution's purpose is subverted. Behaviors are not aligned with the institution's professed goals; rather they are skewed to preserve the rank, power, salaries, and security of rank-holders. The boss promotes not those best suited to the job, but those whose advancement strengthens his own hold on power. Nepotism, favoritism, and cronyism are all examples of institutional rank abuse.

Working for an employer who pulls rank is an exercise in dissimulation and subterfuge. Accommodating such a boss takes a toll on one's health and productivity and adversely affects the bottom line. A few of the many websites that deal with workplace abuse, discrimination, and bullying are listed along with the related readings at the end of this book.

Imagine the effect on those in charge if companies, hospitals, schools and universities had websites for posting complaints regarding abuses of rank and power. Instead of gossiping to a few sympathetic friends, where exaggeration and distortion are expected and forgiven, complainants would have to argue their accusations carefully and accurately or find them ignored.

Of course, challenging the demands of a boss is risky. The goal of most employees is to get through the day, keep their own counsel, give no offense, and hold on to their jobs. When a boss's primary loyalty is to himself, his employee's loyalties are to themselves. Massaging the boss's ego is the first order of business, instead of advancing the company as a whole. Lip service is given to others' concerns, but in truth they are seen as ciphers — disposable and replaceable. Institutional rank abuse skews the judgment of both management and employees away from organizational goals to self-aggrandizement in the first case, self-preservation in the latter.

Rank abuse is a progressive disease. Nonprofit organizations often undergo an evolutionary process that begins with trying to "save the world" and ends in attempts to save the jobs of those who set out to save the world. A telltale sign of this is the pursuit of grants that are not aligned with the organization's goals. Each incremental shift of purpose is rationalized, but in reality fundraising is often driven by the need to maintain lifestyles to which the once-idealistic founders have become accustomed.

On Productivity

Today, the inefficiency of slavery is obvious, but to George Washington, himself a slave owner, it came as a discovery. While on a visit to Philadelphia, Washington noticed that free men there could do in "two or three days what would employ [his slaves for] a month or more." His explanation that slaves had no chance "to establish a good name [and so were] too regardless of a bad one" was that of a practical man concerned with the bottom line, not that of a moralizer, and therefore all the more persuasive.

Today, employers are not dealing with slaves, though it is sometimes argued that wage-earners are wage-slaves and salaried employees are only marginally more independent. Negative motivation — once fear of the whip, now fear of demotion or job loss — is being dwarfed by the positive motivation that comes from being part of a team of responsible professionals. Eliminating deficiencies of recognition in the workplace is proving to be as good for the bottom line as eliminating nutritional deficiencies was in the past for the productivity of day laborers.

As rank abuse is identified and reduced, individual energy is engaged and mobilized. People who feel recognized as individuals and who feel they have a fair chance at promotion give their companies their best. Companies that figure out how to give their workers a voice in management and a stake in earnings reap measurable benefits.

A system of management in which power is abused is vulnerable to competition from one unburdened by the inefficiencies inherent in such practice. In time, the alternative system will demonstrate its advantage by out-producing the first; it is now commonplace for young upstart companies to put older inflexible ones out of business. Invariably, the cause can be traced to calcification of rank. Whether in a firm or state, abuses of rank are self-limiting and, though it may take a while, ultimately self-defeating.

The corporate face of rank abuse is arrogance, none more so than of the monopolist who owns a market and can dispense with good service. Such organizations act as if they "own" both their customers and employees. The truth is they own neither. Hegemonic companies are now learning that smaller, more agile ones can suddenly threaten their existence. Nokia, a Finnish enterprise, came out of nowhere to transform the mobile communications business. Apple and Microsoft did the same in the computer industry. Microsoft was subsequently tried under anti-trust legislation for using its muscle to prevent upstarts from doing what *it* had done on its way up.

The sub-optimal performance of organizations beset with rank abuse provides a conceptual bridge that links morality and pragmatism. As George Washington's observation suggests, slavery's Achilles' heel was its inherent inefficiency. As a system for organizing work, slavery is counterproductive and simply loses out competitively. Perhaps that is what the prophets presciently intuited several millennia ago. They foresaw that certain behaviors and practices were inherently impractical and self-defeating. They labeled these "immoral," anticipating that over time economic and social forces would conspire to bring about their elimination. In this view, the term "moral" does not make reference to some separately existing universe of goodness as set forth, say, in holy writ or as divined by seers, but rather is of the nature of a forecast based on close observation, intuition, and extrapolation. The prophets are seen as astute and brilliant futurists with an uncanny knack for the long view.

Despite their practicality in the long run, moral precepts are often ignored in the near term. Until results show up on the bottom line, we're not convinced. Before rank abuse can be targeted in principle as racism now is, it must first be widely and convincingly demonstrated that it reduces flexibility and adaptability and thereby handicaps group performance and productivity. In this respect, reform comes more easily to businesses than to educational institutions because businesses have the quantitative feedback of the marketplace to inform and guide them.

"Because I say so" management of the firm — as of the family — is on the way out. Moreover, employees now know that obedience does not ensure job security. "Yes men" are a doomed species. People don't want to work at companies that don't permit them to be true to themselves and afford them opportunities to make a difference.

As it becomes clear that more powerful alternatives exist, the burden of proof shifts to those who argue on behalf of traditional, autocratic, top-down management. Gradually, as rank abuse is identified and curtailed, knowledge-guided decision-making displaces authoritarian management. Organizations in which rank is used properly incubate a superior power. Right makes might, not vice versa.

The Intel Example

Intel, like many technology firms, operates with the explicit understanding that any employee is free to challenge any other employee's professional scientific views. A newly-hired twenty-year-old can question a director of research, or the CEO. The policy of open, free exchange regardless of rank is seen as a vital part of keeping the company a creative, productive place.

Intel's legendary leader Andy Grove famously worked out of an open cubicle like everyone else, and had no reserved space in the company parking lot. If he had gotten the customary preferential treatment, those would have been innocuous forms of rank-pulling, not worth objecting to — the latter arguably justifiable on the grounds of sparing him time. Grove certainly could have had such perks if he chose to, so the question is, why did he refuse them?

When *Time* named him "Man of the Year" in 1997, Intel employees whimsically put up a sign at the parking space nearest the building's entrance reading "Reserved for Time's Man of the Year." Such appreciative humor shows a high level of awareness of the purpose of rank and the cost of misusing it. Intel's parking policy is a symbolic expression of the company's commitment to limiting the power of rank so undue deference does not dampen creativity. Abuse of rank is perceived as a threat to good research. Condescension and arrogance are out. Open, reciprocal interaction is valued over pride of position.

Making the distinction between its proper and improper uses revalidates rank where it has been earned and proven within a particular domain. When rank is understood to have a specific jurisdiction, it becomes synonymous with stature. Presidents, CEOs, leaders of every kind gain their rightful, due respect — no more, no less. The only real boss is a better idea or a better question.

On Learning

Until it is understood why so many students who begin school with hope and enthusiasm wind up turning off or dropping out, educational reforms, whether progressive or conservative, will continue to disappoint.

There is a reason that prior reforms have fallen short of expectations, but like the proverbial fish in the bowl, we're too close to see it. The truth is that students do not give their hearts and minds to learning because there's poison in the "bowl." Not enough to kill all the fish, but enough to stunt the growth of many.

This strength-sapping poison is the real and imagined threat of rank abuse, and it pervades all our educational institutions from kindergarten through graduate school. Finding and holding one's position within the hierarchy takes priority over all else. Before students can focus on their texts, they must master the subtext that governs their rank within the school. Whether we give ourselves to the educational enterprise or withhold ourselves from it is determined by our strategy for maintaining dignity within the school hierarchy.

The situation encountered by those who rank low in the hierarchy is emotionally equivalent to that faced by blacks under Jim Crow. Low rank carries a stigma — you're seen as a nobody, and you become vulnerable to insults from teachers and fellow students. It is not a coincidence that the same labels have been used to denigrate students as those for African-Americans: "lazy," "stupid," "uppity," "troublemaker."

Nowhere is the distinction between rank and its abuses more important than it is in an educational context. After all, one function of education is to help us determine a vocation commensurate with our abilities. Seeing how we measure up — or rank — against traditional standards of excellence is a useful tool for guiding us toward specialization. As has been stressed before, there is nothing inherently abusive or discriminatory about rank, or about a fair process of ranking. Doing away with rank is no more feasible or desirable than doing away with race or gender. Not so obvious is rank-based discrimination, and the fact that it is no more legitimate than race or gender-based discrimination.

The problem is that most ranking processes, instead of serving a neutral diagnostic function, have pernicious side effects: they stigmatize those who rank low and exalt those who rank high, and these rankings then become self-fulfilling prophecies. The young are especially vulnerable to rank-based discrimination. It feels to them like a sentence from which there is no appeal, and the effects are apt to compound. In just a few years a debilitating gap can open up between students destined for success and those who are marked for failure.

No child — no human being — is expendable. Everyone has something to contribute, and when that contribution is made and acknowledged, he or she feels like a somebody. Helping individuals to locate that something and then learn how to contribute it is the proper business of education.

We have become alert to the negative consequences of racism and sexism in education, but we are still largely oblivious to the costs exacted by abuse and discrimination based on rank. The reason schools fail to enlist students wholeheartedly in the vital enterprise of learning can be traced to the prevalence of this undiagnosed malady. Both students and teachers are suffering its ill effects. Pupils find themselves resisting and rebelling, not learning; teachers find themselves hectoring and disciplining, not mentoring.

Hearts steeled against the inequities and affronts of rank abuse close the minds of students to learning. So long as the dignity of either pupils or teachers is vulnerable to insult — overt or subtle — educational reforms will win neither their good will nor their best effort.

Today's schools are vestiges of a world that needed legions of workers to carry out laborious, repetitive tasks. Now, however, we find ourselves on the threshold of an age of information and technology that holds the promise of liberation from drudgery. The educational transformation this requires will be as profound as the one launched by nascent democracies two centuries ago when they realized that their survival depended on what Thomas Jefferson called "the enlightenment of the people" and adopted universal compulsory education. The schools built to serve the needs of the manufacturing age trained a literate workforce that could follow directions and carry out tasks that called for little or no initiative. Real creativity was neither expected nor desired from either blue or white-collar workers. Such conformist schooling can take us no further. It is quite inadequate to the needs of knowledge-based societies in the age of information.

As early as 1925 the American philosopher and educational reformer John Dewey argued that a healthy process of self-governance was at least as important as efficiency in political decision-making. If citizens were not actively engaged in making large social decisions, those decisions would be inherently flawed. His reasoning applies equally to learning. Soft-pedaling the workings of rank and power in the learning process is a disservice to students because it leaves them ill-prepared for the future they face.

It's hypocritical to declare that "All men are created equal," and then invest inequitably in the schooling of the young. The impoverished education of many children and the obstacles that block their ability to catch up lock many into permanent nobody status. The loss to individuals is incalculable — the loss to society unimaginable.

I'm reminded of my grade school pal Gerald. He stands out in my memory because from our first sums in kindergarten to high school algebra, we competed in mathematics. For more than a decade we were like tennis rivals who improved each other's game.

Gerald's parents owned a chicken farm. They had immigrated from Germany before the war and spoke English with an accent. In the 1940s this did not endear you to your neighbors or to the school authorities.

What was the result? I had always been expected to go to college and graduate school, and I did. Gerald was expected to sell the eggs produced on the farm, and today he drives a truck that supplies supermarkets not far from where he grew up. Although we showed no significant difference in our abilities, I was encouraged to continue with mathematics and science, and he was not.

At a high school reunion a few years ago, I asked Gerald whether he regretted not developing his talent for math. There were several of us gathered around and everyone present remembered the rivalry between Gerald and myself. With an unmistakable wistfulness, he explained that it had always been assumed he'd work the farm. None of his teachers took his mathematical talent seriously. No one ever encouraged him to aim higher. He never even considered anything beyond high school. I'm sure he could have become a college math professor, and I suspect this would have been more fulfilling and satisfying for Gerald, as well as a more socially productive use of his talents.

Discrimination based on rank is often invisible, like the "nobodies" it targets. It takes the form of recognition for some, but inattention, eclipse, and invisibility for many others, like Gerald. The United Negro College Fund reminds us that a mind is a terrible thing to waste. The waste is more than a personal tragedy. Multiply Gerald by a million and what you have is a dearth of recognition, starvation amidst plenty that goes unnoticed, with the victims taking the blame. Though less visible than shortages of food, recognition famines deserve our attention and warrant relief.

As tyrannies are supplanted by democracies, as police states yield to law-based societies, people grow up. Political maturation goes hand in hand with changes in traditional patterns of domination and submission. Subjects simultaneously reject the paternalism of the authorities, dispense with their own complementary infantilism and victimhood, and assume the responsibilities of citizenship.

Since the collapse of communism, defenders of centrally-planned command economies have become a vanishing species. It seems the flow of information inherent in customer feedback makes for a more efficient regulator of commerce. Though it is now widely accepted that authoritarianism and monopoly lead to economic stagnation, their impact on the educational process remains largely overlooked. It's puzzling how often people who advocate democracy and free markets fail to question paternalism and over-regulation in education.

The competition that protects consumers from shoddy products and poor service is still largely absent in education. There's little variation from school to school, public or private, in curricula or pedagogy. Virtually the same courses are taught everywhere, in the same ways. It's difficult to measure the relative effectiveness of schools because student performance depends more on what students bring with them at matriculation than on what a school does to improve their abilities once they get there. Overarching regional systems of academic certification do more to inhibit experimentation and ensure conformity than to promote quality.

Consumers of most goods and services can take their business elsewhere when dissatisfied; we choose a different brand or shop at another store. But dissatisfied learners encounter obstacles at every turn. I recently overheard a high school student, frustrated with his school's bureaucracy, liken it to the state's Department of Motor Vehicles.

Teachers, professors, and administrators are not the source of education's failures. Most of us, at least once during our schooling, have had a teacher who stirred our soul. Such figures can evoke a love that rivals that for our parents; the educational epiphanies we experience under their tutelage often shape the rest of our lives. The real problem in education lies not with teachers, but with the bureaucratic monopoly within which they work. We are paying the same price paid by command economies — inefficiency, apathy, passive resistance, and obsolescence — for insulating our educational system from healthy rivalry and customer response.

Why has education been exempt from genuine competition and consumer feedback for so long? Because at every level, it's riddled with abuses of rank. While the teacher-pupil relationship that lies at the heart of learning is inherently hierarchical, this presents no problem so long as the teacher's authority is confined to his or her area of expertise and put at the service of student interests. But when administrators and educators substitute their own goals for learners' interests, motivation wilts. Students assume the passive-aggressive posture of the prisoner or slave.

They harden their hearts and close their minds to learning. For many, the game is forfeit from the outset.

The alternative to authoritarianism is not permissiveness, but giving people a voice in governance. The alternative to rank abuse is not an abolition of hierarchy, but a more intelligent, precise, and productive sharing of authority and responsibility. Freeing education from the disempowering effects of rank abuse while simultaneously honoring the experience and wisdom of teachers can transform students into learners and teachers into mentors.

To deliver on Thomas Jefferson's open-ended promise that "all are created equal," we will have to confront issues of the distribution of power among learners, teachers, and administrators. We will have to uproot the invalid uses of rank that educational institutions have blindly absorbed from the societies they serve.

Changing the balance of power is always controversial, as the history of women's suffrage demonstrates. The idea of free elections was once considered treasonous (and still is in police states). Securing the vote for African-Americans all but tore the United States apart. The right to learn will be to the twenty-first century what the right to vote was to the twentieth — the next step in the extension of human rights. The indignities of today's schools keep many from acquiring knowledge and skills, much as eligibility requirements and poll taxes once kept many from voting. To make learning a universal human right will require a transformation in education no less profound than the political transformation that was required to universalize the right to vote.

On Leadership

How dreary to be somebody!
How public, like a frog
To tell your name the livelong day
To an admiring bog!
— Emily Dickinson, American poet (1830–86)

I don't want to go around pretending to be me.
— Philip Larkin, English poet (1922–85)

In any institution, rank-based discrimination limits the access of potentially high performers to better jobs by inhibiting movement between ranks. It also puts those holding high rank under the kind of stress that gradually undercuts the creativity that brought them success in the first place.

Somebodies have jobs and titles and reputations. They enjoy the prestige that comes from serving society as professionals and exemplars. They must have answers and they must perform.

For many somebodies, there's a period shortly after their initial success that's almost like being in love; they're center stage, presenting whatever it is that got them out of "Nobodyland" and made them into a somebody. During this "honeymoon," they constantly show and tell, explaining themselves and their contributions again and again.

This process gradually separates somebodies from their creative source, depleting them until they become empty shells. With enough repetitions, they begin to wonder whether they have anything new to offer. Once the bearer of a gift, they end as its slave. No sooner do they feel fake than others begin to find them boring. Burnout is *the* occupational hazard of somebodyness.

I spent my final months as a college president play-acting the part. I felt like an impostor. Six years of attending committee meetings, faculty meetings, trustee meetings, and alumni meetings had taken their toll on my enthusiasm for leadership. I couldn't stand the thought of becoming — in Yeats's telling phrase — a "smiling public man."

Long before I left the job, I was yearning for time to think, to compose myself, to make myself over. I still acted like a college president in public, but I was impersonating a former self.

Another price that somebodies must pay is knowing that among those who are congratulating them for making it up the ladder are some who can't wait for them to fall off. The German language has a special word for this — *schadenfreude* — the malicious enjoyment of others' misfortunes. The degree of *schadenfreude* is proportional to the resentment that accrues if a disparity appears between status claimed and status earned.

Ninety-nine percent of public attention goes to a handful of leaders, celebrities (both famous and infamous), heroes, and supposed geniuses. The recognition gap between somebodies and nobodies mirrors the economic gap between haves and have-nots. The flip side of the public's obsession with celebrity is its resentment toward those receiving all the attention.

Another danger leaders face is the deference their status induces others to grant them. While making individuals conspicuous, fame paradoxically offers them an escape into a kind of anonymity; fans don't actually know their heroes as individuals or make real demands on them. Folksinger Joan Baez has said, "The easiest kind of relationship for me is with ten thousand people. The hardest is with one."

We do somebodies no good when we cease relating to them as fallible human beings. To keep from stagnating, everyone needs honest interaction with others free of the evasions and flattery accorded those of high rank. Most somebodies suffer irreparable harm from the loss of honest coequal friendships. Exempt from the school of hard knocks, the rich often do not get the kind of feedback that compels them to correct their weaknesses. The fawning courts of Louis XVI and Mao Zedong accelerated their departures from reality. The same can be true of a boss, a department chairperson, or an artistic director. Without continuous accurate response, somebodies are deprived of the living truth they need to continue their personal development. Applause meters, polls, top-ten charts, and bestseller lists are poor substitutes for honest individualized feedback.

The honors, prizes and other perks showered on somebodies often divert them from getting on with their real work, and maintain them in public life beyond the point where it's good for either them or us. Once the lionizing begins, political, intellectual, and artistic somebodies are deprived of the give-and-take with peers that originally stimulated their creativity. As their names gain luster, their work falls in quality, until suddenly everyone notices and they become has-beens overnight. George Bernard Shaw quipped that he could "forgive Alfred Nobel for having invented dynamite, but only a fiend in human form could have invented the Nobel Prize."

When the famous do not coast on their early success, but excel time and again through meticulous preparation, they deserve the same recognition they got the day they first won our hearts, if not something extra for not letting us down afterwards.

In centuries past, royalty had a brilliant mechanism for keeping a king from falling prey to his own image. It was to appoint a court jester whose job it was to remind this supreme somebody that he, too, was a nobody just like everyone else. Only the jester had license to tell the truth without losing his head. He functioned as an escape valve, giving voice to what everyone else knew but could not say. Today, this purpose is served by late-night comedians and dignitary roasts.

Historically, the transition from autocracy to democracy has gone hand in hand with ordinary people coming to see themselves as potential centers of initiative and power. Kings were stripped of their divinity and then of their temporal authority. For a time, we even chopped off their heads to make the point. Now we savage them in the media, reminding them that we realize they are ordinary people like ourselves. Just as attitudes toward royalty evolved, so are attitudes toward somebodies of every sort evolving: from worship to fealty, from fealty to esteem, and from esteem to a fond appreciation for peers who are temporarily playing public roles.

Notably, in recent times, several royal figures have themselves been midwives to democracy. Spain's king, Juan Carlos, facilitated his nation's transition to democratic government after decades of authoritarian rule, even intervening to quash a reactionary coup. Likewise, Nepal's late King Birendra voluntarily gave up near-absolute powers to foster democracy in his nation. Royals can exert a moral force that encourages their subjects to assume the responsibilities of self-government. Their function too can evolve — from the temporal business of day-to-day governing to the symbolic, quasi-spiritual role of embodying their nation's civic virtues.

Attachment to somebody status is ultimately as futile and self-defeating as resignation to permanent nobody status. Somebodies who can't get down off their pedestals turn into statues. Becoming somebody is indeed nobodies' business; but equally, taking a turn as a nobody can be a somebody's salvation.

Fans don't boo nobodies.
 — Reggie Jackson, member of baseball's Hall of Fame (1946 –)

On Spirit

When I taught physics at Columbia in the sixties there was a senior professor in the department who was known for his caustic advice to younger colleagues on how to play the academic game: "It's not enough for you to succeed," he would say sardonically. "Your colleagues must fail." Later, I discovered that his precept came from Genghis Khan's rules of war. Given that most lives of exploration and research include numerous somebody-nobody cycles, the advice is, at the very least, shortsighted. The professor who gave it had been a junior member of a team of physicists whose senior members received the Nobel Prize for research done by the entire group.

Though Americans regard the pursuit of happiness as a social right, we seek it as individuals, each in his or her own way. This is because our passions are personal and unique. They grow out of our questions, our fears, and the contradictions we experience with other people, with others' work, and with society. Initially we wonder: Who's right? What's beautiful? What's fair? What's true? We're not sure. We try this and that. Even after we've found an answer, it's the energy we draw from the inquiry that generates the passion which sustains us as we take our solution public.

If the struggle for survival demands all our attention and resources, we must suppress this kind of exploration. Like the great majority of our ancestors, we devote our lives to putting food on the table. But once survival is assured, issues bubble up into our consciousness.

The late writer Wallace Stegner said, "The guts of any significant fiction — or autobiography — is an anguished question." The same is true of our lives. At the heart of every life lies a question and, like the heroes in novels, many of us recall exactly where we were and how we felt the moment it first struck us. Our questions generate our individuality. Through our response to them, we define ourselves, we become someone in particular. Long before we're even aware of them, they shape our every move. A question generates a quest and a quest crystallizes our identity, transforming us into someone who, regardless of how others see us, we experience as a somebody.

In the core of our being, we all feel open and vulnerable, even when others view us as a somebody. In those places where we're most alive, we are questions, not answers. These change as we age. One has to listen carefully, again and again, to detect new ones, which usually announce themselves in a whisper. At any age, our questions define our growing edge. So long as we've got even a single one, we're not dead. If all we have are answers, we might as well be.

In medieval myths, knights-errant undertook a quest and then lived it to the ends of the earth, often rescuing damsels in distress along the way. As Carolyn Heilbrun has pointed out, until recently women were held to be ineligible for "questing lives." Rank, social and otherwise, still keeps both women and men from cultivating their questions into life-altering quests. But if we can identify our questions and find ways to pursue them, modern-day quests can be as demanding and exciting as chivalric ones ever were.

Chapter Four

THE HUNGER FOR RECOGNITION

"And you are...?"

The question "Who am I?" is one of our basic existential queries. Although many live satisfying lives without answering it, there is a variant of this question that's ubiquitous and unavoidable. That question is "And you are...?"

In our early years, it takes the form "What are you going to be when you grow up?" When we are young adults, the question becomes an inquiry about our social or institutional ties, our job or vocation. In our maturity, it can feel like a request for our résumé.

Our answer to this question marks us, labels us, ranks us in others' eyes. It divides us into somebodies and nobodies.

Somebodies are sought after, given preference. Nobodies are disregarded; their calls are not returned. Most of us have felt like a nobody at one time or another. How others treat us, and we them, hinges on relative rank more than we care to admit. Everyone knows at some level that this is how things work, no one is happy about the situation, and most of us are reluctant to talk about it.

We have spent the last forty years refracting identity through the prisms of race, gender, age, sexual orientation, and so on, but have yet to examine ourselves and our relationships with respect to rank. When we looked at ourselves through the lens of race, we saw injustice. When we looked at ourselves through the lens of gender, we saw inequity. When we look at ourselves through the lens of rank, what we see is indignity. As discussed in the preceding chapter, the indignities that result from the abuse of rank cost us dearly in productivity, in learning, and in the quality of our interpersonal relationships.

A nameless ache pervades the body politic. It is not so much new as it is something we are becoming more aware of as other more prominent pains subside. Once our physical survival and that of our children is assured, concern goes to the survival of something less tangible. We think of it as our identity. Just as our body is sustained by food that compensates our labor, our identity is sustained by the recognition we receive from others for the contributions we make to them. As physical needs are met, the kind of hunger people feel most acutely is the hunger for recognition.

Recognition as Identity Food

Close! Stand close to me, Starbuck; let me look into a human eye; it is better than to gaze into sea or sky; better than to gaze upon God. ...this is the magic glass....
– Herman Melville (1819 – 1891), Captain Ahab addressing his first mate in
  Moby Dick

Before we're born, we're striving to be. Before we know it, we're striving to be somebody. Our personal struggle for recognition parallels our struggle for life itself.

Recognition is to the psyche what nourishment is to the body. It's identity food. The sentient gaze of another human being confirms our very sense of being. That's why solitary confinement is torture. When I see you seeing me, I feel that I exist. When I see you seeing me see you, we exist. Without a "magic glass" to mirror us back to ourselves, we lose our sense of being human.

The cry of a baby commands a dance of mutual recognition that nourishes child and parent alike. Children demand it from adults, and make their parents' lives miserable until they get it. Adolescents show off for their peers, take insane risks, do whatever it takes to set themselves apart, to make their mark.

A federal official writes:

> Going from eighth grade to freshman year in high school was traumatic for me. I was awkward, skinny, and had poor social skills. Almost from the beginning, I was teased by the other students, both boys and girls.
>
> One of my most vivid memories is of getting so frustrated that I started to hit one of the jocks. The other guys had to pull him off, or he would have really creamed me. Shortly after that, I went trick-or-treating with these guys at Halloween and, taking a dare, I threw a lawn chair on someone's porch, just to be accepted.
>
> One thing I did to make myself noticed was carry a $100 bill to school, show it to everyone, and then tear it in half.
>
> I also had an act where people would point their finger at me like a gun, say "bang, bang," and I would moan and groan and fall over in a death agony. At least I was noticed. I'd even do it while driving, throwing my arms out the driver's side window and flopping down the outside of the car door for as long as I could without losing control of the vehicle.

In the film *On the Waterfront*, Marlon Brando plays an ex-boxer and dockworker who has passed up his big chance in life by throwing a fight he could have won. In a climactic scene, he laments:

> You don't understand! I could have had class. I coulda been a contender. I coulda been somebody. Instead of a bum — which is what I am.

A prizefight provides a stark metaphor for the struggle for recognition: the winner is a somebody, the loser a nobody. The contenders are ranked by the outcome — one up, one down. The crowd cheers as the winner raises his fist in victory over his prostrate rival, defenseless on the canvas. A boxing match is a reenactment of the primeval struggle for survival in which the winners took all, dispatching the losers and seizing their property and womenfolk. Although our ancestors could not avoid such brutal competitions, today such behavior is unlawful and increasingly uncommon.

While today's contests for recognition may be more genteel than those of our predecessors, they are no less important. Our achievements, accomplishments, the positions we've held — these are what go on our résumé. Make the team, earn a degree, hold an office or a job, win a promotion, raise a family — any or all of these are the stuff of recognition. It is as their composite that others see us and we see ourselves.

The will to contribute arises from an ingrained sense of responsibility — to ourselves, our fellow humans, and posterity. If we do not contribute something to others — make ourselves *public* in some way — a part of us dies. To be invisible is to be deprived of even a chance for recognition. As the early psychologist William James put it, "The deepest principle of human nature is the craving to be appreciated."

We seek recognition as acknowledgement that we've fulfilled our responsibility to contribute, and that our contribution has been accepted and appreciated.

Recognition Disorders

Not surprisingly, people who go without the nourishment of recognition suffer serious consequences. If untreated, recognition deficiencies may in fact, like their nutritional counterparts, be life-threatening. Failure to find even a few crumbs of recognition can prove fatal.

The federal official continues:

> I often think of Tommie T. I may have had a tough time, but he suffered bullying several orders of magnitude worse. Fat and ashamed, he could not stave off the attacks. I remember kids putting pats of butter down his shirt collar in the lunchroom. He just sat there crying, not defending himself.
>
> While I survived, Tommie's high school experience probably killed him. He ended up working at a lumberyard, never moved from the house in which he grew up, and became a recluse. The last time I saw him he was almost 50. I stopped by his house and

we talked for a few minutes. He had eczema, was obese, just a miserable creature. He died soon after that. Bullying can be fatal, even without shootings.

As the hunger for recognition mounts, the undernourished may become desperate. An outcast starved for recognition who attacks others or himself is giving expression to the unendurable indignity of feeling inconsequential. A confidant of one of the boys who killed a dozen of their Colorado schoolmates at Columbine High said of his friend, "He was afraid he would never be known."

In an interview, the English writer John Fowles, author of *The French Lieutenant's Woman*, said,

> The sense that you are nothing or nobody can drive [one] to violence and unreason. Through all human history it has been the hidden motive — that unbearable desire to prove oneself somebody — behind countless insanities and acts of violence.

Chronic recognition deficiencies can culminate in recognition disorders (analogous to eating disorders) that are so severe, they take the form of aggressive behavior — even war and genocide. And once the tables are turned and former oppressors seen as "nobodies," consciences are disengaged and anything goes. A simple test for telling if a group of people is in the grip of evil is whether the dignity of people outside the group is completely disregarded. Equally as dangerous as the much discussed gap between the rich and the poor is the dignity-indignity gap.

The quest to restore lost dignity is evident in the phenomenon of "jury nullification." A jury consisting of people who feel that the dignity of a group with which they identify has been insulted may choose to overlook evidence against a defendant belonging to their identity group and acquit in order to assert their collective pride.

We commiserate when Jean Valjean steals a loaf of bread to feed his family in *Les Misérables*. Committing a crime while starved for recognition is not different in principle from stealing bread when starving for food. In both cases, punishment is called for, but prevention lies in understanding and alleviating the conditions that are driving the deprived to acts of desperation.

Somebodies and Nobodies — A Closer Look

We seek recognition all our lives, wherever we can find it — from family, friends, teachers, co-workers, even strangers. We're constantly testing: Am I visible or invisible? Valued or discounted? Connected or disconnected? Insider or outcast? Respected or ignored? A somebody or a nobody?

Obviously, no one is a somebody or a nobody in the unequivocal way that someone is male or female. Depending on circumstances, we may feel like a somebody or a nobody from one minute to the next. We may be a somebody in the eyes of one person and turn around to find someone else treating us like a nobody. Once one acquires it, high status is clung to. But the vicissitudes of life ensure that sooner or later, almost everyone gets a taste of what it's like to be taken for a nobody. Loss can make anyone feel invisible overnight — loss of a job, a title, our health, our youth, a relationship.

The knowledge that events beyond our control can change our status — in others' and even our own eyes — accounts for the empathy that many feel toward those of lower status. Disconnectedness, invisibility, and powerlessness — the defining characteristics of the nobody — are not exclusive to the poor, the dispossessed, and the disenfranchised. Everyone is vulnerable to loss, even the rich and powerful.

In the film *Sunset Boulevard*, we sympathize with the faded star who dreams of a comeback. In her plight we see our own, for no matter how well we're doing at the moment, doubts always lurk. It's part of the human predicament that we are all once and future nobodies.

Recognition is not about whether we *are* a somebody or a nobody, but rather about whether we feel we're *taken for* a somebody or a nobody. The willingness of others to acknowledge us is a measure of their respect. Unrecognized, we feel rejected; we're cast as non-persons, pawns in other peoples' employ. Recognized, we count, we matter, we may even find ourselves in charge.

Up and Down the Status Ladder

Nobody in America wants to be a nobody. As a nation, as a society, we're supposed to get somewhere. It's not "Well, my grandfather was a carpenter, my father was a carpenter and I'll be a carpenter." That's very European. Here, everybody is supposed to reach for the brass ring. God forbid you fail.
   – Lowell Ganz (with Babaloo Mandel), Hollywood screenwriters

In aristocratic Europe, everyone had a place. Even those on the bottom had their dignity. It was close to impossible to change your station, but the lowly were afforded some security and respect. In contrast, there's almost no limit to how far you can fall now in the United States. While modern meritocracy affords more social mobility than did European aristocracy, it carries with it the idea that somebody status, once acquired, includes the right to lord it over those you outrank.

In America, where it's possible to make it big, people think, "Why not me?" and fault themselves if they don't at least try for the brass ring. America liberalized entry to the game, but once the game is on, it's winner take all, and if you fail you have only yourself to blame. The price paid for unprecedented upward mobility is the possibility of unprecedented downward disgrace and oblivion.

We're schooled early and sternly in the pursuit of recognition. No sooner do we walk than we're encouraged to "climb." It's in climbing and falling off the ladder of success that we experience "the thrill of victory and the agony of defeat" — in sports, childhood rivalries, class elections, grade point averages, college admissions, dating, and a great variety of other pursuits. In our youth and adolescence we rehearse the "recognition games" that will preoccupy us later.

By the time we reach adulthood and begin to play for keeps, we have a pretty good idea of where we're likely to place in various contests for rank. This foresight influences our choice of which ladders to attempt if we wish to spare ourselves the disappointment, and possibly humiliation, of losing when it really matters.

Typically, we find ourselves climbing several ladders at once, and this improves the chances that our unique combination of talents and training will enable us to climb high enough on at least one to win recognition, to be regarded as a somebody.

When we're competing for the fun of it, winning is not everything. Although public recognition still goes to the winners, our own emotional response hinges on the direction we're moving — up or down — on whichever ladder we're on. If a race has been fair, a runner who does well according to his or her own lights (say, by recording a personal best) is satisfied even though others ran faster. We actually value our competitors as rivals who help us draw the best from ourselves.

But the image of a *status* ladder — with nobodies at the bottom and somebodies on the top — comes disturbingly close to how we see ourselves and others much of the time. Higher rungs signify higher rank and are reached via personal or professional achievement. Our current standing is measured by the rungs below and above us. Looking down from the top are luminaries like the presidents and prime ministers, film stars, Nobel laureates, and CEOs of multinational corporations. No one needs to ask who they are or what they do.

Somewhere about halfway down is a blurry boundary between Somebodyland and Nobodyland. It takes a success of some kind, as in a job or a relationship, to get past the middle rung and be taken for a somebody. There's truth in the popular song lyric "You're nobody till somebody loves you," or the country western line, "I was nobody last night, but I'm somebody today."

When you're below the midpoint, your mother doesn't brag about you to her friends. If a stranger asks, "What do you do?" you have no easy answer. You may take refuge in something you used to do, or divert attention from the hole in your identity with vague generalities or future plans.

While people are understandably reluctant to share information about themselves if they sense it will cause others to perceive them as inferior, they commonly take pains to establish, or embellish, their rank if doing so might bring them advantages. Two examples follow. First, an observation from a leader of wilderness camping trips, who reports that her clients frequently introduce themselves with something like, "In real life, I'm a doctor":

On our trips many guests feel they need to introduce themselves by what they do, rather than by what they like to do. I try to skip the job scenario by asking people about their dreams and hobbies. Even in the wilderness people seem to feel a need to establish their place in the social order, and they do it by talking about how they earn a living.

The second example is from a book editor and illustrates the pride we take in social rank and the shame we feel at its lack.

During my freshman year at college I enrolled in a course in English literature. There were only about 16 students and I was looking forward to the kind of learning experience that a small class would afford. The professor conducted the first meeting in his home. As a kind of "getting to know you exercise" he began with, "I'd like all of you to introduce yourselves and tell the rest of us what your father does for a living." I was dumbfounded. My father was a bus driver. He was a hard-working man and had always taken satisfaction in the fact that he could send me to this prestigious school without even a request for financial aid. Knowing that he was proud of himself and of me, and that suddenly I felt ashamed of him, made the shame doubly acute. One by one the students introduced themselves and followed with their glamorous pedigrees: "My father is a dean of Harvard Medical School." "My father teaches at Temple." "My father is an attorney." As my turn approached I felt my mouth getting dry. I simply couldn't bear to tell the truth. I introduced myself and followed with a quick "My father is a transportation engineer."

Despite their diversity, nobodies have a number of shared characteristics. Their common predicament is invisibility. Their common desire is respect. Their common need is to connect. Take as an example women who arrange for a hiatus from work to stay home with their children, and then feel abandoned by their former colleagues. One of them writes:

I left the "working world" from the time my first child was born until my second entered preschool. Except for nap times, stretches without the children were rare. We couldn't afford babysitters on one salary. Once in a while we'd manage to escape and attend parties given by my husband's co-workers, most of them young and childfree. At first I looked forward to getting out into the adult world again, but soon I began to dread it because of the inevitable question, "And what do you do?" Having never before worked so hard, on call 24 hours a day and overwhelmed by the demands of two toddlers, I began to resent being made to feel apologetic for being "just" a mom.

Connections are what set somebodies apart from nobodies. Somebodies have them, while those of nobodies are tenuous, if not completely lacking. When a secretary guarding the somebody in an inner office asks "Who are you with?" she's probing for your connections in order to evaluate your rank. Good connections deter people from treating you like a nobody because they indicate you have allies, that you are not alone. They testify to recruitable power and so command respect.

From a political consultant:

> At Washington cocktail parties people ask what you do for a living during the first 30 seconds of the conversation. When I was Executive Director of a national nonprofit working on transportation safety issues, I was of no interest to the would-be movers and shakers. They would simply walk away from me (sometimes without even a contrived exit line).
>
> But when I started working for a news organization, things changed. Because the media is considered to be a second god to government, a shadow power unto itself, these same people suddenly gave me their full attention. Similarly, when my wife became a producer for *All Things Considered* at National Public Radio, people started to give her attention in a way they never had before. Some of them even started "playing me" in the hopes that I would help them get to her.

The Ins and Outs of Nobodyland

Newcomers to Nobodyland often think they're alone. Actually, the place is crowded. It's just that nobodies don't usually declare themselves — some because they want to be left alone, others because they're ashamed. But the impulse to hide away keeps nobodies weak. They're reluctant to stand up for themselves, and only as a last resort do they stand up together. Rather than unite, nobodies typically turn on each other. Those who've suffered abuse because of their rank become abusers themselves.

An Englishman living in the United States:

> I had occasion to visit the Social Security Administration and could hear that blacks at the head of the line were being treated disrespectfully. I was about to attribute this to American racism when I realized that the civil servants behind the counters who were dishing out the insults were themselves black. It doesn't make much sense to call denigration of this sort "racism," but that's how it would be described if the bureaucrats were white.

An Israeli television producer makes the point in another context, and shows what can be done to counteract the abuses of bureaucracy:

> Israeli immigration officials often misuse their powers, particularly on Russian immigrants. This is especially sad because Russians were trained under the Soviet system to believe that an official is the master.
>
> Israel is the only country I know of where immigrants receive counseling in how to cope with abuses of the bureaucracy they must negotiate. They are taught not to cringe and disappear or give up when officials try to fob them off.
>
> In my work as a television producer, I see the same kind of thing, and I have an equation for it: the lower their rank, the more people abuse members of society who are even weaker than themselves. Frustration and feelings of inferiority fuel this cycle of destructive behavior.

The fact that nobodies often do unto others what's been done to them goes a long way towards explaining why they have remained disconnected and disorganized, isolated and weak.

Unless people are either obviously valuable or dangerous, somebodies tend to treat them as if they don't exist. A woman, recently turned 50, writes:

> Talk to any woman over 50 and she will tell you that there is a certain pain that comes with becoming invisible. It happens at around age 45. You realize how much of the way you are related to is based on sex appeal, and suddenly you are treated impatiently — ignored, unseen.

I know of a group of women who joke about exploiting "post-menopausal invisibility" by robbing banks. Many men over fifty, in the decline of their careers or possibly even downsized and out of work, find themselves washed up on the lonely shores of Nobodyland as well.

Slights delivered on the basis of rank are not only tolerated, they're expected — just as in times past, "good ol' boys" established their credentials by peppering their speech with racial slurs. While race and gender-based epithets are no longer acceptable, it's still open season on nobodies. "Nobody" is the ultimate epithet of dismissal, implying not merely low status, marginality, and expendability, but no identity whatsoever. Not worth taking into account. Of no consequence. Invisible. Nothing. Zero.

Lack of fairness in the pursuit of recognition is experienced as an insult to dignity. Dignity denied rankles, then embitters. People without it are like people without food. They think of nothing else. People who aren't allowed to compete, are arbitrarily assigned a false rank, or are otherwise systematically handicapped seethe in silence until one day they either combine forces with others like themselves in protest, or they give vent alone to their repressed outrage and suffer the consequences.

For those who simply give up and accept the world's view that they are indeed nobodies, Nobodyland becomes a sorry prison. Feeling they have nothing left to lose, they may retreat into a private misery or proceed to make life miserable for others. Either way, the suffering of the nobodies in our midst radiates outward in ever-widening circles, like the sound waves of a tolling bell.

But there are many who, despite the travails of Nobodyland, never lose heart. They may suffer indignities but they resist seeing themselves as losers. For such people, Nobodyland can serve as a way station from one identity to the next.

The Parade of Invisibles

Victor Hugo immortalized the down-and-outs of nineteenth-century France in *Les Misérables*. Ralph Ellison's *Invisible Man* suggests a latter day parallel — "The Invisibles." The twentieth century witnessed a procession of one group of Invisibles after another gaining recognition on the world stage.

In the nineteenth century, the labor movement demonstrated to workers that power lay in numbers. By the mid-twentieth century the Jewish people — to whom most nations had turned a blind eye during the Holocaust — compelled the world to give them a homeland. The postwar years also saw millions of unrecognized colonial peoples raising the flags of newly sovereign states throughout Asia and Africa.

The civil rights movement ended the invisibility of black America. Since then, women, seniors, people with disabilities, farm workers, gays and lesbians have also demanded recognition. The century that began with these groups in the shadows ends with them in plain sight. Hugo and Ellison would be astonished.

As part of the Parade of Invisibles, whole categories of people have been treated as nobodies: racial, religious, and national minorities; the infirm and the elderly; welfare mothers, the homeless, the downsized; students, children, and — always — the poor. Those denied recognition were branded "kikes," "niggers," "Chinks," "spics," "retards," "dykes," "fags," "crips," "spastics" — until they organized and started marching. Once they found their voice, they became visible as human beings. With visibility came the power to change not only how others addressed and treated them, but even how others felt about them.

Although it is no longer considered socially acceptable to ridicule people with disabilities, the following two examples illustrate the indignities they still suffer. The first is that of a young male construction worker with a hearing loss, as described by his wife:

> There are many carpenters and supervisors on the job and there's a lot of banter. Due to his hearing loss, Mike is left out most of the time, but he does fine one-on-one, where he can use lip reading in addition to his hearing aid.
>
> One journeyman he works with, who knows Mike needs to see peoples' lips when being spoken to, purposely turns his face away and mumbles while giving Mike directions, and then gets mad if Mike asks him to give them again. Mike has often gone ahead without really understanding his instructions out of reluctance to ask the journeyman to repeat himself. He is no less capable than the others, but working with them is exhausting and humiliating for him.

The second example is from a young woman with cerebral palsy who is training to be a therapist:

> People are always telling me what to do. Older women will see me outside and say, "Where's your coat?" I know it's due to my disability. Respect doesn't come easily. I often feel dismissed when someone without a disability wouldn't be.
>
> At work people think it's OK to belittle me in front of others. My boss calls me "sweetie" and "honey," but when I do something she doesn't like she's quick to criticize.
>
> Often employers have acted as though they were doing me a favor by hiring me, and then used that as an excuse to pay me less. Once I get an advanced degree and have a private therapy practice, I think this kind of discrimination will disappear.
>
> What really brought the importance of a higher degree home to me was a dissertation I read on physically disabled women whose children were taken away from them by state agencies. In every instance, the women who lost their children were poor and uneducated.
>
> I simply couldn't not be in school. If I'm middle class with an academic job, then nobody will be able to take my children away.

Through history, the strong, the powerful, the wealthy, and the titled have tended to regard those they dominate and control as interchangeable pawns. While nobodies have lost many skirmishes, they have also won some world-changing victories.

Paradoxically, the price of gaining collective visibility is often a blurring of individuality. Like Ellison's protagonist, many of those belonging to groups in the Parade of Invisibles that have won acknowledgement and respect continue to feel invisible as individuals. So, too, do a considerable number of spectators who have watched this procession from the sidelines — people who have felt a surprising kinship with the marchers based on something deeper than race, gender, or nationality. It's a connection rooted in the near-universal human experience of isolation and non-recognition, derision, and dismissal. Nobodyness is everywhere, and everywhere veiled in shame.

Chapter Five

THE SOMEBODY MYSTIQUE

The Bricks and Mortar of Consensus

Our social relationships are shaped by laws and rules and moral attitudes that, taken together, constitute a social consensus. One such consensus was the "separate but equal" policy of segregation; another was that regarding the proper roles of the sexes. It was difficult and dangerous to challenge either of these tacit agreements until the late twentieth century.

A social consensus is a well-defended edifice built of "bricks" and held together by "mortar." The bricks are the laws and politics that form the building blocks and the mortar is the mindset, or psychology, that holds them all together. Both political and psychological changes are required to dismantle such an agreement.

Typically, psychological change precedes a political assault on the status quo. Not until a great many individuals conclude that something is wrong and that an alternative exists will they organize politically and try to bring down an existing edifice. Those willing to try something new need not always be outspoken champions, but they must at least have detached themselves from the old. Only when enough people arrive at this state can the existing consensus collapse and a new one rise in its place.

Until the 1960s, the social agreement on gender roles was taken for granted. Its bricks were the laws and rules that limited women's opportunities and enforced the status quo. The mortar was the belief that females were the "weaker sex." In dubbing this belief the "feminine mystique," Betty Friedan and others set in motion the deconstruction of the edifice that was sexism.

Creating new expectations and attitudes regarding women's roles prepared the way psychologically for Title IX of the Education Amendments of 1972 prohibiting sex discrimination in educational institutions receiving federal funds. "Consciousness raising" was the name given to the process that loosened the mortar of sexism.

Segregation, too, was a structure that had to be disassembled brick by brick. This meant replacing the extensive body of racist laws with new civil rights legislation and discrediting the prevailing beliefs of white supremacy.

Replacing the consensus that supports abuse of rank will likewise require new bricks and mortar. If anything, the task will be even more difficult than for sexism or racism because rankism underlies *all* forms of discrimination, and is more deeply entrenched.

The political component of rank-based discrimination — the bricks — consists of the whole interlocking body of civil law, institutional by-laws, governance procedures and traditions that make it difficult, if not impossible, to challenge the well-defended and often overextended authority of those in positions of power. Currently, this power shields individuals of high rank from the merit-based evaluations faced by those "lower down" who might otherwise challenge them for a fair share of the pie.

Legislative change marks a late stage in the process of consolidating a new consensus. Then follows a long period of testing in the courts. Proving discrimination — whether it be racism, sexism, or rankism — is invariably a complex, arduous task. We should not expect otherwise. Open-and-shut cases are rare because often it is pure rank that is operative, and not any abuse thereof. In that event, the "discrimination" exercised is in fact discernment, not prejudice, and charges of unfairness are unwarranted.

In this and the following chapter, our concern is primarily with the psychological dimension of the social consensus that supports abuses of rank. By analogy to Friedan's coinage, we call this the "somebody mystique."

The process of dismantling the segregationist consensus and deconstructing the feminine mystique, and the ways in which resistance was gradually overcome, provide a preview of what will be involved in overcoming the abuse of rank. The endeavor is likely to take several generations. People do not give up power until they either find themselves confronted with greater might or see a dignified role for themselves in a new configuration.

Why We Put Up With Abuses of Power

I have mentioned several reasons for the existence and the persistence of the phenomenon of rank abuse. First and most fundamental, rank is linked to power and power protects those who hold it. While a position of authority may have been earned at the outset, one can often maintain it not through continued demonstration of excellence, but rather by simply using that authority to fend off would-be challengers. In this sense, rank can secure a kind of tenure for itself.

Secondly, titleholders can extend their influence illegitimately to areas over which they have no right to rule. This happens when rank earned in a limited domain is used to impress or intimidate and thereby expand its reach. If performance is not subject to periodic review, somebodies on top can be spared the consequences of ill-serving nobodies below them. High rank inhibits protests and shields perpetrators.

What, then, could be more natural than to seek high status for the perks and protections it offers? This is, ironically, one of the reasons we tolerate abuses of rank. We covet the rewards that come to the somebodies of the world, so we're willing to endure a lot for a shot at the life we see them leading, even if that shot is a long one. Should we, by hook or crook or sheer luck, acquire fame and fortune, then we too could insulate ourselves from the cruelties of life. What's more, we might even the score with all those who ever looked down their noses at us. "To the victors go the spoils" is the proverbial formulation. For winners, the rewards can be great indeed.

On a different note, we often tolerate a measure of corruption because we believe that hierarchy, and the abuses that it invariably entails, is the price we have to pay for social stability. Rank is fundamental to hierarchical organization, and hierarchy enables us to cooperate. It is therefore understandable that we sometimes put up with the misuse of power out of fear that otherwise we'd suffer the consequences of disorganization, perhaps even fall into anarchy.

Yet another reason we put up with abuse is related to the kick the dog syndrome. We sense that we're not entirely innocent of pulling rank in our own dealings with other people, and do not wish to be held accountable ourselves.

"Life isn't fair" is the mantra of paternalism. We're schooled to believe that unfairness is a fixture, that incivility and injustice are ineradicable. "Isn't rankism just part of human nature?" people sigh, resignedly.

One of the hard-earned lessons of the twentieth century was that racism and sexism are not innate to human nature. While it is virtually inevitable that a power advantage will be exploited initially, it is just as inevitable that such abuse will eventually be resisted. In this sense, any particular kind of rankism is no more immutably part of human nature than are racism or sexism. If anything, it is human nature to *resist* abuses of power. Racism, sexism, and rankism may be entrenched and hard to uproot, but they are not carved in stone. The first two have been put on the defensive, and the third — rankism — is no more likely to survive scrutiny than its discredited kin.

The ultimate argument people use against the idea that rankism is a problem is to deny its very existence. In this view, efforts to eradicate abuses of rank are seen as attempts to abolish rank altogether, in the name of some ideal of utopian egalitarianism.

But to depict opposition to rank abuse as a "leveling" of individual differences completely misses the point. Eliminating the wrongful uses of rank actually restores *earned* rank to its rightful, respected place—not by the blurring of differences, but by targeting exploitation. Eliminating rank would indeed be egalitarian, but in the absence of an alternative to hierarchy as an instrument of management, it would be self-defeating. When rank is abused, the result is an insult to dignity. Therefore, eliminating rankism is *dignitarian*, not egalitarian.

To propose that the answer to abuses of rank is getting rid of rank would be analogous to proposing that we deal with racism by getting rid of racial differences, or that we eradicate sexism by getting rid of differences of gender. That critics come to such absurdity suggests they may be looking to kill the notion of rankism in its cradle — but then, the powerful are usually not keen to do anything that might undermine their position. The truth is that rank abuse can be culled like weeds from a garden while leaving the many varieties of plants flourishing, each in its own distinct ecological niche.

The world has never lacked for reasons to ignore protests from targets of discrimination and unfairness. The victims have been called "lazy bums," "malcontents," "special pleaders," "incompetents," "unqualified," "ungrateful," or "whiners." So too must the low in rank brace for categorical dismissal of their claims. Privilege's defense will be to smear the very concept of rankism by distorting its meaning, denying its existence, or insisting that it's nothing new. But those who have felt rankism's humiliations know differently.

Once we grasp the distinction between the proper and improper uses of rank, it becomes possible to take up the problem of rank abuse directly and attack it in all its guises. This amounts to nothing less than removing all unfairness, wherever it can be shown to exist, on the grounds that its cost to society as a whole outweighs the benefits to incumbents.

At every point in our social evolution, power rules. Abuses of power persist until the individuals or institutions perpetrating them find themselves facing a greater force. This would be grounds for cynicism were it not that when power is abused, it is misused; and when it is misused, there eventually surfaces a fairer, stronger alternative. Once this is found and implemented, it supplants its predecessor. The long-term trend of this evolutionary process is the discovery of ever more effective forms of cooperation, successively out-producing, out-performing, and displacing authoritarian institutions.

This argument could be dismissed as circular — as was Darwin's "survival of the fittest" initially — were it not for the fact that there is by now a long list of abusive practices that have invariably proved to be inefficient. The "de-selection" of rankist organizations is analogous to the de-selection of relatively unfit organisms in the struggle for reproductive survival in a given ecological niche. Darwin's principle is not circular (fitness can be defined independently of survival), and since it can be foreseen that the inefficiencies of rankism inevitably handicap organizations burdened by them, the notion that rankism is recessive is not circular either.

Once a less rankist, more democratic organization has been conceived and institutionalized, it prevails over those that, through their abuse of power, have become debilitated and vulnerable. This, of course, is the reason that dictators and monopolists go to such great lengths to avoid competition. By the time rivals win a chance to challenge them openly and fairly, the powers that be are usually far weaker than the alternatives they have been suppressing, and they succumb quickly. The transition, once it begins, often occurs overnight, as it did in Romania, the Soviet Union, Indonesia, and Serbia.

The same factors that predispose us to put up with rank abuse disincline us to question the somebody mystique, at least until something happens to us personally that forces us to do so. The women's movement demonstrated that when it comes to changing a social consensus, the personal is political. Since everyone's personal history is unique, everyone's path to political awakening is different. For most, the will to challenge a prevailing social agreement is born of the suffering they themselves have experienced while endeavoring to be part of that agreement. Following is a description of my own journey from the personal to the political. It may help illustrate the process of traveling in and out of Nobodyland, but can be skipped by anyone who prefers to stick with the more general themes of this book.

Nobody, Too

I'm nobody! Who are you?
Are you nobody, too?
Then there's a pair of us—don't tell!
They'd banish us, you know.
    – Emily Dickinson

There were about thirty pupils in my second grade. Most of our parents were prosperous, but about twenty-five percent of my classmates were poor, their families working small farms in rural New Jersey. Every one of us was white, so race did not figure in how our teacher, Miss Blecher, treated us. But class differences, as revealed by the clothes we wore to school, did.

Arlene was one of the poor children. She wore the same faded plaid dress every day. She was very tiny and thin and spoke in a whisper. Most of us bounded onto the school bus, but Arlene struggled up the steep steps, averting her eyes and sitting by herself.

The first thing our teacher did every morning was inspect our fingernails. One day Miss Blecher told Arlene to go to the hall and stay there until her fingernails were clean. I wondered how Arlene would be able to clean her nails out there, without soap or water. Later, filing out to the playground, we snuck glances at her. She must have heard the snickering as we passed by — standing alone, slumped against the wall, hiding her face, trying to make herself invisible. A nobody.

I was unaware of it then, but in retrospect it's obvious that our social ranking in the community largely affected the attention our teachers gave us in school. Overall, the status we brought with us to school on our first day — something that was far more evident to our teachers than it was to us — was preserved intact upon graduation.

If our parents were prosperous, we were destined to replicate their success. It was Miss Blecher's job to perpetuate this order of things. When I had difficulty, my mother asked to see Miss Blecher and soon she was giving me extra attention.

Miss Blecher probably had no idea how future ability is shaped by self-fulfilling expectations based on social rank. She was an unwitting accomplice to the up or down escalators we were riding as we began second grade. Without realizing the extent to which our rankings on day one had been determined by our experiences at home and in previous classes, she perpetuated them through subtle but systematic patterns of preference and disfavor. Since her time, it has become widely recognized that if our parents, teachers, and friends assume we will fail, then we are likely to do so. In contrast, if a child has lived with success and it is expected of him or her, continued success is all but assured.

In my teens, I was witness to black kids suffering this kind of humiliation, but I chalked it up to racial prejudice. The color difference threw me off the track of what was really going on — exploitation of the power difference embedded in the prevailing racist consensus. But for a series of experiences three decades later that gave me a personal taste of Arlene's daily lot, I doubt I would ever have realized that the abuse suffered by her and by blacks had a common source.

After college and graduate school I took my new Ph.D. to Columbia University where I taught physics. I climbed the academic ladder in the usual way until, in the spirit of the sixties, I volunteered to teach a science course to kids who had dropped out of Seattle's predominantly black Garfield High School. The challenge was to prove that these young men, whom the system had failed, could indeed learn under the right conditions, with the right assumptions.

Learn they could and learn they did. The key, I discovered, was that before they would accept any teaching from me, I had to give them something else: recognition. Before they would listen to me, I had to listen to them. They had been taken for nobodies all their lives, and they would not accept my authority until I communicated to them that what they thought mattered to me.

I did this by teaching only what they said they wanted to know. *Their* questions would determine the curriculum, and I would stop the moment I detected boredom and move on to whatever they said they wanted next. Since they all had different interests, this meant shifting topics when even a few became restless. If hanging out on the street was more appealing than what was going on in class, they were free to get up and leave.

The first day began with a lewd question. It continued with the students yelling out more questions — on sex, drugs, race, justice, and death — which I followed like a soccer ball bouncing around the field of knowledge. I interpreted inattention as a signal to return the ball to the students.

When I didn't know enough to respond to a query, I would say so, brush up before the next session, and answer it if it came up again. I found that when the pupils were asking about things they cared about, they kept asking until they were satisfied.

You might wonder if such a process would ever lead into areas like science or philosophy. By way of an answer, I recreate an exchange that took place one day. It began, as did everything in the course, with a question.

"Why do we always get busted for smoking pot while college kids get off free?" After heated discussion, I raise an issue that seems to lie beneath many of their comments: "Is it better to be black or white?" Silence. I follow up: "Is it better to be black if you live in Africa?" A chorus of "Yeahs."

When I press them to elaborate, attention turns to the deficiencies of American justice as they know it. They see second-class citizenship as a consequence of living in a white society. When the storm subsides, I ask, "Are there any *other* advantages of dark skin in Africa?" Leroy shouts, "No sunburn." Raucous pride fills the room.

And then out of nowhere comes the best question any student has ever asked me. Michael hollers, "So how come everyone isn't black?" I have to tell them I don't know, but that night I search my old biology text for an explanation. At the next class I explain that fairer skin transmits more light, which enables the body to utilize vitamin D, which in turn protects against the crippling effects of rickets. The higher your latitude, the less ambient sunlight, so in northern climes it is fair skin that holds the biological advantage.

At the end of the semester I tested the students on everything we had covered, and discovered that virtually all of them retained nearly 100 percent of it. Everyone who had started the class earned an "A" (except one boy who was killed by his father halfway through the semester). They had not only learned, but more importantly, they had learned that they *could* learn. And they'd discovered they could do so without giving up their dignity, which made them feel powerful. Many of them returned to regular classes and graduated. Years later one or another of them would come up to me on the street, introduce himself, and tell me that the course had changed his sense of who he could be and what he could do in the world.

What students need in order to move from the path of resistance to the path of cooperation is a taste of somebodyness. They will open their hearts and minds in return for recognition.

Without this experience, I would not have become involved in the reform movement that was then sweeping higher education. One thing led to another, and a few years later, I was appointed president of my alma mater, Oberlin College, a liberal arts college in Ohio.

Nothing on my résumé would have gotten me the job if I had not also been a tall white male. Image counts for a lot in choosing people for leadership roles. The singular importance of height struck me when, just before taking office, I attended a conference of academic presidents. Except for the fact that they were all white, it could have been a reunion of ex-professional basketball players.

Height is so tied to rank in people's minds that it deserves a brief digression. Among males, it confers a kind of rank all by itself, and lack of it can be a source of considerable suffering. This vignette comes from a friend who is a (tall) mathematician:

> As a faculty member I was on a doctoral committee with several other professors examining a graduate student in physics. It was his final hurdle to the Ph.D., and his career hung in the balance. Just a few years earlier, I'd been in his shoes. There is probably no scarier moment in one's entire education, unless it's the first day of kindergarten.
>
> The young man was less than five feet tall. At one point he ran out of space on the blackboard on which he was writing equations and asked if he might erase some of what he'd done. The chairman of the committee, pretending to be helpful, suggested, "There's still plenty of room at the top — just climb up on a chair," and he directed the nervous candidate to fetch one from the back of the room.
>
> The student turned red, carried a chair to the blackboard, and climbed up on it to complete his presentation. As a last rite of initiation, he'd been made to look and feel like a schoolboy. The committee chairman smirked condescendingly behind his back, and looked around to see if the rest of us shared his delight in the fellow's humiliation.

Age, not height, was my problem at Oberlin. I soon found out that at thirty-three I was too young to be trusted by the faculty and too old to be trusted by the students. For the next four years "controversy" was my middle name. The introduction of co-ed dorms made the cover of Life magazine. Sports journalist Howard Cosell reported a "first" on national television when the predominantly white college hired several black head coaches. Other reforms were covered in the national media. Everything I did was scrutinized and discussed by the Oberlin community.

In 1970, every college campus in the country was in turmoil over issues of race, gender, and student autonomy, all against the backdrop of the war in Vietnam. It was in dealing with racial integration and the changing status of women that I began to understand the pivotal role of power differences in sanctioning prejudice and sustaining discrimination.

At exactly that time, for reasons that had to do with age and maturity rather than race or gender, most college students were also in revolt against what they felt was unwarranted adult supervision. They were no longer willing to accept college authorities patrolling the dormitories and acting as substitute parents. Teaching young black men in the high school in Seattle had revealed to me the depth of pupils' yearning for recognition, dignity, and a measure of autonomy. Now, these college students were demanding control over a whole range of social and educational issues. "Ageism" joined "racism" and "sexism" in the lexicon as a new and different kind of discrimination.

When the smoke cleared, colleges everywhere had revamped many of their policies. Some dormitories had become co-ed; course requirements had been relaxed; interdisciplinary courses and majors had been introduced. In fact, about all that remained untouched was the non-representative governance structure that had failed to respond to the impending crisis in the first place.

In 1974 I left Oberlin's presidency with the three contemporaneous revolutions — race, gender, and age — very much on my mind. It would not have been hard to arrange another position of comparable status, but I knew I had to take some time off. Nonstop politicking had left me bruised and burnt out, and I knew that if I was ever to do anything creative again, I had to come to a complete halt and reeducate myself. When I finally tried to get back into the game after a few years of travel and study, my attempts at reentry resulted in a string of unanticipated indignities.

Late one Friday afternoon in 1978, it finally hit me: I was in Nobodyland! I was waiting near a public phone in New York City for a promised call that never came. My spirits sank as five o'clock approached. I had driven to New York from California, arriving on a Monday, and had spent the week trying to revive some old connections to the world of foundations where I hoped to win support for a new project. By half-past four that Friday, the business day all but over, I faced the weekend with all my leads exhausted.

As a former somebody in the world of academia, I knew how easy it was for those who know the right people to get support for almost anything. I had helped arrange jobs, sabbaticals, and grants for others, often with just a call placed by my secretary. I had traveled on an expense account. Now, without a position or title, I was getting a taste of what it was like to be a nobody.

During the week, when former physics colleagues asked what I was doing now, I saw their eyes glaze over as I tried to explain my project. Because it lacked institutional backing, nothing I said sounded real to them. Their reactions to my changed circumstances ranged from polite curiosity to ill-concealed pleasure at my apparent misfortune. Soon they were sneaking glances at their watches, looking for an opportunity to usher me out of their offices, suggesting that we have lunch *next* time I was in town. In the eyes of my former physics colleagues, I was a nobody.

Just a few years prior I was in a position to bestow favors; now I found myself begging for one. Somebodies' secretaries would inquire who I was with, expecting me to legitimize myself through affiliation with an organization. Defiantly, I'd announce, "Myself!"

Though I'd concealed the fact that the number I'd left with their secretaries was that of a public phone, while standing in the booth I had the creepy sensation that the somebodies I was hoping to hear from could see me waiting there, fending off other nobodies who might tie up the line. That Friday afternoon I let go of the last remnants of my former status. In a sobering flash, I saw myself as my onetime associates were seeing me—as a nobody. It was then that I remembered Arlene, standing in the hallway all those years ago feeling invisible, rejected, and humiliated.

Over the months and years that followed, I came to understand that it takes position to get position; that low rank, or loss of rank, can handicap a person in the same way that race, gender, age, or disability do. Discrimination based on rank bars nobodies of whatever stripe from a fair chance at becoming somebodies, and keeps somebodies in their public roles long after it's good for them or anyone else.

The Genesis of the Somebody Mystique

O body swayed to music, O brightening glance,
How can we know the dancer from the dance?
— W. B. Yeats, Irish poet and playwright (1865 – 1939), from *Among School Children*

There is something more than the promise of perks, the fear of retribution, or the specter of anarchy that keeps people from objecting to the abuse of rank. Challenge it, and you're likely to be dismissed as a loser, charged with lacking respect for authority, or labeled a "leveler." Support it, and you're a team player, "one of the boys," an "organization man."

The somebody mystique cements an unconscious rankist consensus. Dazzled by images of the rich and famous, we are distracted from the injustice of social inequities by infantile envy and longing. The public is offered vicarious pleasure in the spectacular successes of a special few, in lieu of a fair chance at individual fulfillment. Why are we so vulnerable to the somebody mystique? How does it work its magic?

When we witness true excellence, our hearts swell with admiration and respect. The somebody mystique is grounded in the awe we naturally feel toward those who have *earned* high rank — rank that is excellence-based. But once we experience this, something else happens, something mysterious. Our focus shifts from the accomplishment to the person, from the art to the artist, the dance to the dancer.

The somebody mystique evolves out of our childhood perception of our parents. When we are young, we see mom and dad as superior beings. In adulthood, the reverence we have for them is transferred to contemporary authority figures and celebrities, who then, too, seem superhuman, beyond reproach, even above the law. It's reassuring to have "gods" among us, to touch the hem of their garments as once we reached for our mother's skirt.

Fame itself becomes our focus, more than the human being who possesses it. People see icons instead of ordinary mortals like themselves. Somebodies acquire an aura that seems to make them special, superior, even sublime. It's as if they give off a radiance that lingers in psychic space like an echo of the divine right of kings. Psychiatrists call this phenomenon "transference." Anthropologist Ernest Becker called it "the spell cast by persons."

From *MAD Magazine* comes this pointed question referring to a series of Mr. Coffee ads featuring Joe DiMaggio.

> In the course of his 16-year career with the Yankees, Joe DiMaggio hit 361 home runs, had a lifetime batting average of .325, and hit safely in 56 consecutive games. Which of these accomplishments qualifies him as an authority on coffee makers?

Celebrity endorsements gain their currency because of the somebody mystique. If someone is good at basketball, that does not make him or her an authority on breakfast cereals, trucks, telephone companies, or fragrances. Winning at war does not, in itself, qualify a general for a leadership role in academia or politics. The movie star who promotes a candidate is trading upon rank earned in one realm for credibility in another. In all these cases, however, we have no one to blame but ourselves. Ultimately, it is we who expand people's power beyond the confines of their initial accomplishments; it is we who buy the products they represent; it is we who put them in office.

Our adoration of somebodies is such that it may cause us to forsake all objectivity. We cease to question their actions; we hesitate to insist that they play by the same rules as we do; we cut them slack. Under their spell, we are persuaded to acquiesce in our own indignity. Just as women colluded in maintaining the feminine mystique that held them down, so do we participate in maintaining the somebody mystique that keeps us all in our place — usually gazing upward.

Somebodies enthrall not only those of lower rank, but also one another. I once stood in the Oval Office, a witness to the meeting of two somebodies of the seventies: President Jimmy Carter and pop singer John Denver. What I remember most about the encounter was their looking starry-eyed at each other! Having prestige themselves does not immunize people to the siren song of the somebody mystique. Even the most successful seek to bolster their own status by keeping company with others of high rank.

The collapse of the racist consensus in this country ended white monopoly on power. Simultaneously, the eye-opening slogan "black is beautiful" marked the beginning of the end of the monopoly that whites had on beauty. Likewise, the erosion of the feminine mystique led to the breakdown of traditional notions of gender roles and responsibilities. We should not be surprised if dispelling the somebody mystique changes our values and politics just as profoundly.

Chapter Six

DECONSTRUCTING
THE SOMEBODY MYSTIQUE

Why should we demystify somebodies? We love our heroes. We worship geniuses. We're fascinated by celebrities. Why not leave them on their pedestals?

The idea that "somebody knows" is reassuring, comforting. Long before we discover that our parents and teachers are neither omniscient nor omnipotent, we are introduced to historical figures — religious and political leaders, scientists, and artists — who replace them in our adult imaginations. We leave school with the impression that these cultural icons are superhuman, a breed apart that stands in relation to us as we do to chimpanzees.

But excessive fascination with somebodies can interfere with our own mature pursuit of due recognition. Up to a point, role models are useful in this enterprise, and so are heroes. They open our minds to what we might make of ourselves. But if we idealize and romanticize them, or focus on the symbols and rewards of their success, we miss the real story. Instead of simply adulating famous persons, we should try to understand the conditions that allow for their emergence.

This means we must disenthrall ourselves with the somebody mystique. Imitating the hero's lifestyle does not give us his or her powers. Artists who rent garrets in Paris and writers who hang out at the

Algonquin Hotel do not thereby further their creative endeavors. When children play dress-up, they are preparing themselves for adulthood. When adults do it, they are mistaking lifestyle for life.

Dispelling the somebody mystique will require the creation of a new understanding of somebodies. Just as we are weaned from our parents, so must we demystify our idols if we are to realize ourselves fully as adults. In neither case does this mean disparaging those upon whom we have been dependent.

Before taking up the task of deconstructing the somebody mystique, let us first take a brief look at the constructive role of heroes in the development of our identity and our choice of work.

The Function of Heroes

Not every age is an age of heroes. In order for there to be such larger-than-life figures among us, there must be great social causes, such as just wars or liberation movements that call for extraordinary leadership. Otherwise there are no heroic niches to be filled, and we look elsewhere — to business, sports, entertainment — for people to admire.

Of late there appears to be a paucity of heroes, and what few there are seem pallid in comparison to those of yesterday. None approaches the stature of a George Washington, Thomas Jefferson, or Abraham Lincoln, a Susan B. Anthony, Franklin D. Roosevelt, "Ike" Eisenhower, or Martin Luther King, Jr. Perhaps this is because the challenges we face at this historical moment are not of comparable grandeur or gravity to the ones in which those individuals found themselves. As Admiral "Bull" Halsey, Commander of the Pacific Fleet during World War II, said, "There aren't any great men. There are just great challenges that ordinary men are forced by circumstance to meet."

Fortunately, we need not restrict our search for heroes to the present. Those from the past or, for that matter, from fiction, can serve our needs as well as, if not better than, the living.

Wherever we find them, heroes are exceptional somebodies. They are people who inspire us, people we emulate, human templates on whom we try to pattern ourselves. Their lives instruct us by illuminating the qualities we must develop in order to respond to challenges, perhaps not so unlike the ones they faced. We study their stories for guidance in dealing with our own predicaments. The examples set by Lincoln, Churchill, and Gandhi, and in our own time by Nelson Mandela and Mother Teresa, influence millions. Unsung heroes, whose remarkable qualities may be known only to us — such as an aunt, a grandfather, or a neighbor — can be even more valuable sources of guidance and instruction.

As our problems change, we seek out new heroes to show us the way. One generation's nobodies may be somebodies to the next, or the other way around. Paths pioneered by the few allow all of us to fix upon the right course in a fraction of the time it took them to discover or carve it out. Hero worship, like love of any kind, provides a mechanism for absorbing the ways of others.

Idolatry can be orchestrated by the state, in support of autocracy. Glorification of individuals also functions to redistribute the labor force. The prestige enjoyed by scientists in the fifties helped draw many youngsters — myself included — into scientific careers, actually producing an oversupply by the late sixties. In recent decades, following in the footsteps of our new cultural icons — the cyber-millionaires — the young have flocked to computers.

Anyone's success can stir us to reach beyond our own limitations, to attempt and sometimes accomplish things we had not thought possible; it can function as a stepping stone to the realization of our full selves. But to move from admiring disciple to self-actualization, we must transcend the simple worship of others. Idolization substitutes fantasy for reality and amounts to shirking one's responsibilities. The cult of personality, on the part of either an individual or a society, keeps us from growing up.

In order to dispel the somebody mystique, we must learn to see our somebodies for who they really are—no more, and no less. Until we do, we diminish the chances of fulfilling our own legitimate aspirations to be somebodies ourselves. In misperceiving how heroes, geniuses, and celebrities gain recognition, we lose the opportunity to understand how they manage to make the contributions that originally bring this recognition, and how we might do the same. We reach our full maturity and stature when we see ourselves in our heroes and find our heroes in ourselves.

The Inside Story

About Genius

> *Masterpieces are not single and solitary births; they are the outcome of many years of thinking in common, of thinking by the body of the people, so that the experience of the mass is behind the single voice.*
> – Virginia Woolf, English writer (1882–1941)

Geniuses are our "heroes of the mind." They are somebodies who offer us both inspiration and understanding in matters artistic or intellectual. Since relatively few works of art meet the test of time and most scientific hypotheses prove false, we might infer a rarity of genius from the rarity of *works* of genius. However, what is far more likely is that any number of individuals could have served as vehicles for the landmark creations and discoveries in the world. It is the *opportunities* for making great discoveries that are the rarity — not the people capable of doing so.

At any historical moment, there are only so many significant leaps we are capable of making because we are limited by our current set of beliefs. In the sciences progress results from noticing things that deviate from our expectations. Thus, any advance requires that we first have in place a conceptual framework from within which such a discrepancy can emerge. Great discoveries — which bring their makers somebody status — depend on a large body of previous work done by relative nobodies. Our reluctance to accept this notion is a measure of the power of the somebody mystique.

Breakthroughs in science and in art are almost always a consequence of someone being in the right place at the right time, asking the right question, and then having the right skills to answer it. It's rather like putting the last few pieces into a jigsaw puzzle. Countless others have contributed, but only science and art historians are interested in all the experimentation, missteps, the tearing apart and rebuilding that precede the triumphant act of completion. The public reserves its praise for finished masterpieces. When, after a long process, someone adds the final few touches or last key ingredient and produces a new synthesis, we declare him or her to be a genius.

The history of physics shows that at the time Einstein published his special theory of relativity, others were very close to achieving the same result. Einstein was the first to put all their results into a consistent framework through a creative synthesis based on an important new idea. But historians agree that if he hadn't discovered the key to relativity when he did, then within a few years, someone else would have.

A realistic understanding of Einstein's contribution is far more useful than the glowing accounts that make him a godlike figure mysteriously creating a whole new world with the wave of his pen. As young physics students, my friends and I all wanted to be like him. When I began my graduate studies at Princeton a few months after his death, he was regarded as a deity. The older among us who had seen him at seminars and the lucky few he'd invited to tea regaled us with stories of the great man.

Long after he'd ceased to hit any jackpots, Einstein kept trying to unify the laws of physics, but he was no more successful than others. Similarly, after Darwin published his theory of evolution, his work did not stand out from that of the other researchers who then flooded the field, drawn by his seminal insight. Their next order of business was the more routine, elaborative work of applying the theory of natural selection to existing unsolved problems. Contemporary examples of this phenomenon abound in the arts as well. Musicians, for example, may strike a vein of gold which then runs dry. Works of creative genius depend on a conjunction of the right person with the right set of skills and the right historical context.

In 1921, a prediction of Einstein's general theory of relativity was confirmed experimentally during a total eclipse of the sun, making him the first modern world-renowned scientist. At this point he could easily have been seduced by celebritization, but he knew his rank had been earned in physics and physics alone, and instinctively avoided the accompanying enticements of fame — declining, for example, the presidency of Israel.

In the arts, too, we can see that "genius" results from accumulation and collaboration. In her prescient feminist masterpiece, A Room of One's Own, Virginia Woolf argues that writers like Jane Austen, the Brontë sisters, Chaucer, and Shakespeare gave final voice to the work of many forerunners. An artist I know makes the point more crudely: "All artists are pickpockets."

This is true of creative work of every type, including politics and business. Steve Jobs — who oversaw the development of the Macintosh computer, which "borrowed" much of its technology from earlier research done at Xerox's Palo Alto Research Center— admits that his very motto, justifying imitation, was plagiarized from Picasso: "Good artists copy; great artists steal. Genius is the art of hiding your sources."

The French writer Paul Valéry (1871–1945) believed that it takes two to invent anything:

> One makes up combinations; the other recognizes what is important in the mass of things which the former has imparted. What we call genius is much less the work of the first than the readiness of the second to grasp the value of what has been laid before him and to choose it.

In this passage, Valéry is simply acknowledging the collaborative nature of originality. Every invention owes its existence to a lineage of others reaching back into prehistory. Most of the earlier steps are unknown and unrecognized. But we can be sure that some ancient tribe put an embryonic form of democracy into practice long before any political philosopher ever wrote down its tenets. Some alchemist stumbled upon a chemical principle that now bears an academician's name. And some amateur fiddler or flutist composed a tune that lies at the heart of a well-known symphony.

Michael Jackson acknowledged that the "moonwalk" he made famous was learned from Brazilian street kids. Some famous people understand and admit their debt to their predecessors, but many do not, and the public, in its craving for heroes, downplays this debt. What is said of saints in Islam is perhaps also true of geniuses: The greatest of them are unknown. Today, the Internet, by making it possible for widely dispersed individuals to stay abreast of the latest research and to post their own results, is taking collaborative research to a higher level. A blurring of the distinction between somebodies and nobodies cannot be far behind.

In the world of business, deal-makers and networkers specialize in finding the last pieces of a puzzle and putting them together. Although some CEOs are certainly better than others, success in the corporate world is invariably a group effort. We tend to attribute company success to the brilliance of a single executive (and overblown compensation packages reflect this view). But such people are very much the beneficiaries of circumstances and timing — of occupying a niche where their knowledge and skills match their organization's needs at a particular moment in its growth.

None of this is meant to deny the existence of great talent or leadership. No matter how close predecessors may have come to a particular scientific or artistic discovery that we now admire, the person who achieves fame has mysteriously spanned what seemed to be an irreducible gap. We can call that genius, if we choose, or we can think of it differently. The magical ability to span such gaps is, in fact, familiar to us all. We count on it every day, every time we do or say something we've never done or said before. It's just that most of our personal histories do not situate us at the frontiers of physics, art, philosophy, business, or politics.

An act of creative genius depends upon the conjunction of a prepared mind with the right opportunity. When the preparation fits the situation, discoveries are made. The difference between the persons we celebrate as geniuses and the rest of us is in fact remarkably slight. In no way does it justify either their arrogance or our servility. The somebodies we love most understand this and express it in their equal regard for others.

About Celebrity

The celebrity is a person who is known for his well-knownness.
– Daniel Boorstin, American writer (1914–)

We live in an age of celebrity. Spellbound, we gaze upon the rich and famous as they make their entrances, take their bows, and exit to our applause, unaware that such thralldom diminishes us and is a disservice to those we lionize.

Why do celebrities so transfix us? Like us, they are nobodies in their private hearts. We scrutinize them hoping to catch a glimpse of their foibles and failures — their nobody side. Their lives provide a constant reminder of the difference between the public persona and the private person — the somebody and the nobody — that coexist within everyone. By acting out their public roles while at the same time visibly suffering as ordinary people, celebrities — from rock stars to royalty — exemplify the human predicament and, in so doing, minister to our spiritual needs.

Celebrities with the common touch serve as living reminders that we, too, are not defined by our roles. Those who lack humility may be admired, but they fail to move us. That is why Princess Diana and President Reagan enjoyed the affection of the masses, and Prime Minister Thatcher did not. Diana was "the peoples' princess," her personal pain obvious to all and shared by many. Reagan's informality proclaimed, "I'm president and I'm no different from you." As an actor, perhaps he understood he was not really the "king" we chose him to play for eight years. In contrast, Thatcher came across as haughty.

John F. Kennedy, Jr. inherited his celebrity, and he knew it. His upbringing and good sense protected him from accepting the public's view of him. His outward demeanor showed that he had come to terms with his somebody and nobody roles. In his perspective on celebrity, he contributed something original and important.

Elvis Presley — the "king" of rock and roll — and Marilyn Monroe — the sex "goddess" — both combined nobility and vulnerability. They were loved for revealing so clearly the nobodies they carried within. But they paid dearly for their fame. Being Elvis and being Marilyn destroyed the human beings who played those public roles. Just as the feminine mystique suffocated women, the somebody mystique suffocates celebrities. In its absence we would still admire performers for their talents and acknowledge their contributions, but we'd respect their privacy and not oppress them and infantilize ourselves with our idolatry.

In an aristocracy, high social rank, or "class," mattered more than any other kind of rank, because it carried political power and signified authority over landed estates and the people living on them. The term "classism" is sometimes used to mean abuse and discrimination based on differences of class. As class is a special kind of rank — social rank — so classism is a subcategory of rankism, narrower in scope. In meritocracies, class loses much of its importance, because although it usually still correlates with wealth, it is not directly coupled to political power.

Today, movie stars and other public figures enjoy the benefits of high social rank. But winning any contest has both a payoff and a price. The payoff for fame is that people are glad to see you; when you walk into a room, you don't feel invisible. The price is that most of the people who are glad to see you are glad for reasons that have nothing to do with who you really are.

About Fame

I'm gonna live forever.
I'm gonna learn how to fly.
I feel it comin' together.
People will see me and die.
— Dean Pitchford, lyrics from the musical *Fame*

When a person gains fame, it is like an airplane taking off. The process begins with a long, low-profile run down the tarmac. But once they are airborne, the somebody mystique lifts ordinary people far above the crowd, seeming to offer a lifetime guarantee that never again will they want for recognition. It's a false promise.

Until recently, Ellen was a principal dancer in one of America's leading ballet companies. Now, in her early forties, she writes:

> From the moment I took my first class, I couldn't imagine an existence apart from ballet. With determination, hard work, and a little luck, I was accepted into a major company straight out of high school. Within a few years I was promoted to principal dancer. The sweat and pressure of carrying a performance, which I thrived on, were rewarded with bouquets of flowers thrown at my feet, throngs of fans waiting at the stage door for my autograph, and parties at wealthy patrons' mansions. I was treated like a princess.
>
> But stardom was short-lived. At 29, I had a career-threatening foot injury that sidelined me for six months. Although I recovered, my foot was never the same. Bit by bit the

aches and pains increased, as did my daily dose of anti-inflammatory drugs. I started losing roles, one by one, to young dancers. I realized I should think about a new career, but my identity as a dancer was all I had. My body was failing me, yet my spirit clung to the stage. I realized my days were numbered when the director told me I was "too mature" to dance a particular role on opening night. I was 33. My last years in the company were spent in disappointment over roles lost and anxious anticipation of the inevitable. Still I clung to the only life I had ever known in which I was a somebody.

In the celebrity culture of our times, many believe that unless they're famous, they're nothing. As it turns out, the kind of recognition we need is like the kind of food we need: not just plates of caviar or hot fudge sundaes, but a balanced diet.

Fame is like wealth. Though everyone has heard that money can't buy happiness, few would decline an opportunity to learn this for themselves. But in order to feel like a somebody, we do not need fame or celebrity. For most of us, there is reward enough if we contribute something of ourselves to others, and have that contribution duly recognized. Our appropriate "public" may simply be a network of family, friends, acquaintances, colleagues, and strangers, all with a shared interest. Presenting our work — that is, making a present of it — to even a relatively small group of people meets the need to give of ourselves and communicate our truth; it brings all the acknowledgement most of us need. What we offer can be anything into which we've put care and effort — a work of art, a garden, a cake, a theory, a speech, a thought, a home — you name it. Indeed, naming it is part of what brings it, and us, the recognition that is due.

To seek fame in itself usually takes a toll on creativity. A more productive goal is to strive to do our best. When we can no longer improve significantly upon our prior attempts, then it's time to put the result out into the world. Despite promotional strategies, the ultimate effects of our contributions are more like those of the proverbial messages in bottles drifting out to sea: Where they go and whom they touch are matters beyond our control and, quite possibly, none of our business.

About Success

The public somebody you are when you have a "name" is a fiction...The only somebody worth being is the solitary and unseen you that existed from your first breath and which is the sum of your actions and so is constantly in a state of becoming under your own volition—and knowing these things, you can even survive the catastrophe of Success.

— Tennessee Williams, American playwright (1911–83)

F. Scott Fitzgerald quipped famously that "There are no second acts in American lives" — but he was wrong. Americans love comebacks. We never tire of stories about people who have gotten back on the horse that threw them and regained their stature.

We learn in school that "nobody" is spelled f-a-i-l-u-r-e. What's not so well known is that "somebody" is spelled the same way, except boldly, and in capital letters: F-A-I-L-U-R-E.

No one likes to fail, but failure is a great teacher — perhaps the only real teacher if only we allow it to be. Every setback contains a message that suggests the next step in the process of discovery. The key to escaping from Nobodyland is tenacious persistence guided by the feedback of our errors. Success is almost always the endpoint of a long string of "false" steps and "wrong" turns. Only in hindsight do we see these as having been integral to the creative process. You can't become a new somebody if you're unwilling to be a nobody. You have to be able to tolerate failure and learn from it. Niels Bohr, the father of atomic physics, ascribed his achievements to "making my mistakes faster than others." The ability to bounce back from failure is a better predictor of future success than is the absence of failure.

Perhaps nothing is as harmful to learners as shaming them into excessive caution so as to avoid mistakes. Consider the words of several somebodies who rejected the facade of infallibility and thereby kept on discovering new things:

I think and think for months and years. Ninety-nine times, the conclusion is false. The hundredth time I am right.

– Albert Einstein, German-American physicist (1879–1955)

Results? Why man, I have gotten a lot of results. I know 50,000 things that won't work.

    – Thomas A. Edison, American inventor (1847–1931)

The way to get to the top of the heap in terms of developing original research is to be a fool, because only fools keep trying. You have idea number 1, you get excited, and it flops. Then you have idea number 2, you get excited, and it flops. Then you have idea number 99, you get excited, and it flops. Only a fool would be excited by the 100th idea, but it might take 100 ideas before one really pays off. Unless you're foolish enough to be continually excited, you won't have the motivation, you won't have the energy to carry it through. God rewards fools.

    – Martin Hellman, a discoverer of public key encryption

The reason we so hate to admit a mistake can be traced to our fear of nobody status. We think others value and love us for the faultless personas we present, and feel that any admission of imperfection will lead to rejection. Furthermore, failure activates our sense of shame, so we feel like a nobody to ourselves. Suppressed is the deeper knowledge that we love others and they love us not as perfect somebodies, but as the vulnerable human nobodies we all are. Our shared essence is the capacity for seeing things in a fresh way and for changing in response.

The instinct to defend oneself, right or wrong, is not without higher purpose. No one can tell in advance where new truth lies. The only way to find out is to fight for the truth as you see it. Later, in retrospect, you usually discover that what you thought to be the whole truth and nothing but the truth was in fact only a piece of it. Your opponents had another piece, and it is through synthesis that a more comprehensive and powerful model emerges. The whole truth is reached by combining our piece of the truth with that of others. The argumentative process enables both us and our antagonists to see what is essential in our initial positions and what is idiosyncratic and dispensable, and so to arrive at a new work of greater universality.

But once an error is identified, it's in our best interest to admit it — as quickly and cheerfully as possible — and to move on. After all, it's only a belief or an action that has been found wanting — not us, personally. We remain intact to argue another day, on behalf of another cause, just as lawyers do when they lose a case.

Supporting the creativity of others does not mean allowing sloppiness in the name of freedom or non-interference; quite the opposite. But we intensify our interactions with others fruitfully if we focus on the weaknesses in their *work*, and refrain from attacking them *personally*. Creative people are often simply those with the highest tolerance for going back to the drawing board and trying to improve upon their previous attempts.

Parenting or schooling that stifles such experimentation in the name of always having the "right" answer impedes creativity no less than permissive tolerance of poor work. We remember most fondly those teachers who urged us to take ourselves seriously and then held us to exacting, rigorous standards. Seeing intrinsic worth in us, they encouraged us to be even better than we thought we could be. This explains why we may value a "tough" teacher more than a "nice" one.

In education at its best, we love mentoring from those who make no attempt to conceal their fallibility, permitting students to watch as they make mistakes, catch them, and move on. Once we see how admitting to errors frees one from posturing and opens the way to fresh experience, we have learned the secret of prolonging our own creative life.

Gordon Sherman, onetime president of Midas Muffler, wrote:

> Only when we open ourselves fully to the assaults on our self-esteem that are inevitable when we venture to enact our vision; only then can we understand and even welcome the role of failure in the cycle of eventual success.

The Young Are Disenthralled

Conventional wisdom about the generations says that people who came of age in the 1950s believed in their country and in progress. Those who came of age in the '60s believed in righting wrongs and saving the world. Those who came of age in the '70s believed in saving themselves. And those who came of age in the '80s and '90s believed in getting rich.

None of these goals appears to be working today. Increasingly, the young are demanding that jobs be compatible with inner satisfaction. They are questioning the assumptions of the somebody mystique, and refusing to play by old rules. Millions of them have postponed employment to search for something that offers meaning and value. Many are choosing to extend their stay in Nobodyland.

Like all newcomers, the young are initially seen as a bunch of nobodies or "slackers" by their seniors. But unlike in the past, today's youth seem unconvinced that by subordinating themselves to the current set of somebodies, they'll eventually join their ranks. They are refusing to delay the pursuit of happiness until after they are successful. Instead, they're attempting to shape careers that fit into life, and not the other way around.

As each generation comes of age, it takes a critical outsider's look at those that preceded theirs. The young today accuse their seniors of unbalanced ambition, acquisitiveness, status-seeking, cynicism, condescension to underlings, and a willingness to sacrifice personal life for professional advancement. Like those that came before, they are determined to change the way the career game is played. Unlike their predecessors, however, they are staying out of the game for years, instead of months.

This defiant embracing of nobodyness is reminiscent of the African-Americans, women, and the elderly who seized upon the very trait that had marked them for mistreatment and made it their rallying point. One wonders whether the attitude of today's youth — in the spirit of black pride, feminism, and the Gray Panthers — could be the vanguard of a Nobodies' Liberation.

For those now joining the labor force, slavish workaholism, unfair treatment in the office, and other such indignities are unacceptable. They prefer to hang out on their own, rather than be ciphers within a group whose goals they do not share. They are mobile, resourceful, multi-skilled, and readier than any generation before them to take their chances. Unlike their parents, they do not give their loyalty to a firm, nor do they expect a commitment in return. Instead, they consider work as a simple transaction: the swapping of time and abilities for money. Groping toward a new set of principles that downplay hierarchy and status, they stand for the notions of equal dignity and a more equitable distribution of rewards.

Young adults today are more likely than their elders were to extend the nobody experience beyond adolescence into the middle and late twenties. If, in their later years, they come to recall this interlude with shame, they may cling to whatever positions they end up in, forsaking the innocence and courage that once emboldened them to put their own creative development first. But if, as seems more likely, the single lifelong career is a thing of the past, this prolonged early experience in Nobodyland might seem providential. In that event, the midlife career crisis, for one, will not be the time of terror and trauma we have come to expect. Rather, it will be seen as an opportunity for rejuvenation.

We've all known someone like Joe, a school friend of mine:

> Joe felt he was fired because his heart was no longer in accounting. His skills were above average, but for some time his performance had been lackluster. When he was passed over for promotion, he began to see himself as others did — as a faceless bean-counter. Then one year, downsizing left him jobless.
>
> His wife wanted him to go back to school, get an MBA, and make himself more attractive to employers, but he resisted. The only thing he really enjoyed was coaching his daughter's soccer team. He'd always been good with kids, knowing instinctively how to get the best out of them. Saturday morning soccer was the high point of his week. Now, with more free time, he began running a program of "midnight basketball" as well.
>
> Joe had always regarded his work with kids as secondary. One day, he caught himself trying, for the hundredth time, to convince himself to return to accounting. In that instant, he suddenly stopped putting his avocation to the side and decided instead to cultivate it — to do what he loved most and to share that with others. He changed course, got a teaching credential and within a few years made the transition to teaching and coaching.
>
> Nobodyland was where Joe realized that something he'd always loved was also something of value to others. By taking it

seriously, he transformed himself from someone who for years had felt like a nobody into someone who feels like a somebody every day of his life.

For every Joe, there's a burned-out teacher dreaming of starting a business or a struggling entrepreneur who is a month away from moving across the country and beginning over. When, like Joe, we catch ourselves discounting our secret dreams, and decide instead to embrace them, we take the first step out of Nobodyland. More and more, the young are doing this routinely, without the guilt and angst that plagued their elders.

The turning point usually comes when we realize we have been overlooking something of significance and value right within us — often something in plain sight. This can occur at any time of life — youth, middle or old age — and it can happen repeatedly. As we grasp the worth of our discovery and begin to act on it, we stop feeling like nobodies. We become the bearer of our unique gift to the world. And we become somebodies again, even if, at first, only to ourselves. Recognition of our new status may take longer, though sensitive observers will at once detect a change in our bearing.

Full acknowledgement occurs when we make our finished contribution. If it's something we're in the process of developing, that may take a while. The time between identifying what it is we have to offer and actually delivering it — and with it ourselves — from Nobodyland out into the world is typically measured in years, sometimes in decades, rarely in months.

In making our way out of Nobodyland, mistakes and failures are road signs, not traffic tickets. Winston Churchill's advice was, "If you're going through hell, keep going." The Irish writer Samuel Beckett (1906–89) had a sign above his desk which read "Fail. Fail again. Fail better."

Chapter Seven

THE QUEST FOR DIGNITY

The struggle for recognition is the motor that drives human history.
– Francis Fukuyama, American philosopher citing Hegel (1952 –)

The DNA of Democracy

Democracy is tough-minded, not utopian. Far from denying the existence of power, democracy prides itself on staring power down. The DNA of democracy can be found in each of its incarnations, from the senate of ancient Greece, to Viking and Native American councils, to the Magna Carta, to South Africa's 1994 constitution.

Oppression is the muse of rebellion. Revolutions are made by people in pain. The kernel of the democratic idea is to limit the potential for abuse of governmental power and the human suffering it causes by limiting the prerogatives of rank. The ultimate mechanism for accomplishing this is to make rank-holders periodically accountable to those under their control. Abraham Lincoln, who believed that "no man is good enough to govern another without that other's consent," coined what has become democracy's mantra: "Of the people, by the people, and for the people."

This essential idea — that holders of high rank should serve and protect people, not tyrannize or domineer them — is surely one of the most subversive of all time. Because of it, we now expect leaders to facilitate and improve our lives, and they themselves speak of being "hired" or "fired" by their constituents.

The past is filled with examples of revolts and revolutions through which nobodies have managed to curtail the prerogatives of the somebodies. Nobodies invariably outnumber somebodies, but are usually held in check by fear of superior force. If they're sufficiently provoked to overcome this fear and act in numbers, the leaders they follow often have had formative experience in both worlds. They've felt the pain and humiliation of nobodyness, but also enjoyed the privileges and protections of rank and acquired an insider's knowledge of the workings of power.

Although the Vikings had trial by jury, a parliament, and a common law tradition (including women's rights) centuries earlier, I'll begin this thumbnail history of the democratization of political power in the medieval English town of Runnymede. There in 1215 a handful of English feudal barons — somebodies to the peasants on their lands — assembled to extract a charter of rights from the one person to whom they were nobodies — King John. In yielding to their demands, the king unwittingly gave the process of democratization a vital foothold.

If the barons had realized their action would set in motion a series of assaults on rank that would eventually bring the nobility down, they might have thought better of it. Antecedents notwithstanding, the Magna Carta signed at Runnymede has come to stand for the right to trial by a jury of one's peers — a basic procedural safeguard against rankism — and, more generally, the supremacy of universal law (applying equally to everyone) over the arbitrariness of autocracy. The restrictions placed by the Magna Carta on the powers associated with rank set in motion an irreversible widening of participation in governance. Its signing represents a seminal victory in the quest for political dignity. The leap from rule by a solitary strongman to an oligarchy of noblemen may seem like a small one, but it was a *qualitative* change — from one to many — and it took millennia. The next step — that from a small group of aristocrats to universal suffrage — was a *quantitative* one, and would take only centuries.

Another turning point in this process was the establishment of parliamentary sovereignty during England's Glorious Revolution of 1688–89. Parliament, an institution that had given a voice to at least some of the people, enacted a bill of rights that further circumscribed the power of the king while simultaneously asserting the rights of citizens. It was a precursor to the U. S. Constitution, with its checks and balances and the attached Bill of Rights. These bills, along with the French Declaration of the Rights of Man, were milestones in the quest for dignity.

Both the Americans and the French were aware that liberty by itself did not ensure human dignity. In 1776, Thomas Jefferson tucked the radical proposition "All men are created equal" into the Declaration of Independence. The slogan of the French revolutionaries — *Liberté! Égalité! Fraternité!* — also had an egalitarian thrust. These two immortal phrases contain the seed of the idea that democracy means universal fairness and equality of opportunity — ideals antithetical to aristocracy.

In his 1835 classic *Democracy in America*, Alexis de Tocqueville described the American passion for equality as an irreversible social vector. Antipathy to favoritism runs deep in the national psyche. Unequal opportunity betrays the idea of fair play and contradicts American ideals.

Jefferson's promissory note obliges us to eliminate injustice in all its various guises. Our representative democracy provides a practical, if sometimes plodding, mechanism with which to redeem that promise.

As historian Garry Wills points out in his book *Lincoln at Gettysburg*, when Lincoln invoked Jefferson's proposition at Gettysburg in 1863, he was implying that all races were included, and must be accorded equal rank.

With every lurch toward fairness, there is an understandable tendency to heave a national sigh of relief and declare that now, with impediments removed, anyone should be able to realize the American dream on his or her own. While admitting that many were handicapped in the past, we like to think the latest changes have ended unfairness, once and for all. Yet for African-Americans, the end of slavery was just the beginning of a very long struggle for equal opportunity. Other newly liberated segments of the populace have also found that much remains to be done after their second-class citizenship is officially ended.

Well into the twentieth century, political rights were privileges linked to traits such as race, gender, and age. Not until the 1960s did we witness a renewed and intense assault on the prerogatives of social rank. Those years retain their emotional hold over us because the events of that decade challenged and transformed the rules governing contests for recognition. Though discrimination still exists, the social consensus that once supported it has now collapsed. The same fate befell the feminine mystique — the reigning ideal to which women were expected to conform until Betty Friedan's book described their predicament, gave it a name, and launched a movement.

The past century was witness to revolutionary changes in historical patterns of recognition, a "psycho-tectonic" shift, if you will, as fundamental to human identity as the rearrangement of our planet's tectonic plates have been to the human habitat. Millions of former colonial subjects now take pride in their status as citizens of sovereign states. Though the idea of freedom under equal protection of the law has yet to take hold within some countries, the overarching political story of the century was the collapse of imperialism, colonialism, and tyranny, and the spread of representative democracy. This extended even to the Soviet empire, which vanished overnight with the collapse of the Soviet Union and the birth of a quasi-democratic Russia. The revolution launched at Runnymede eight centuries ago continues to propagate throughout the world and threaten remaining autocratic regimes.

The idea of democracy has not only spread horizontally across the globe; it has also moved vertically into the social and political structures of democratic countries. One identity group after another has sought and gained a measure of freedom from oppression for its membership. If we look briefly at this process, we'll see how it leads inevitably from the now-familiar liberation movements to an understanding of the importance of rank, and the need for a new movement to overcome its abuse.

Race, Gender, Age, ... Rank

In the decades following World War II, under mounting pressure from minorities and women, Americans gradually accepted the idea that differences in race, gender, and age are not valid bases for discrimination. Racism, sexism, and ageism, all formerly taken for granted, were now considered unacceptable. Millions of people formerly seen as second-class citizens came to expect, and insist upon, equal dignity and opportunity as their birthrights.

But despite these successes, indignity, unfairness, and oppression are still commonplace. What changed was that labels like "black," "female," and "gay" were removed from the list of particulars that, ipso facto, singled out individuals who had one or more of these characteristics for categorical disempowerment and injustice.

Given that opportunity remains unequal, that justice is not blind, that indignity is the daily fare of many, we might well wonder if we've overlooked some other damning trait that could account for such ongoing inequities. Once we go beyond race, gender, age, disability, and sexual orientation, we are led ineluctably to rank.

Rank or status has always been a major player in the struggle for equality, but it was invisible so long as we were focused on characteristics like color and gender — the obvious occasions for prejudice. In fact, rank is the single most important item on our résumé. It trumps all the other traits that usually define our identities. But because of its link to authority, it's a risky subject that is seldom discussed.

Rank is the proverbial rhinoceros in the living room, as sex was in the fifties. It's an embarrassing issue that everyone is aware of but avoids as long as possible. It is the unmentionable on the bill of particulars that can, and often does, lead to the disadvantaging of those who are low on the totem pole. We still live every day with inequities deriving from a form of discrimination that everyone knows but no one calls by name — discrimination based on rank.

On Naming Rank-Based Discrimination

To have a name is to be.
— Benoit Mandelbrot, inventor of fractals (1924 –)

New words are often slow to win their way into the lexicon, especially new isms. When "sexism" was coined in 1968, the valid objection was raised that abuse and discrimination based on the difference between the sexes had nothing to do with sex (in the sense of the sexual act). In fact, if we were to choose a word today, I suppose it would be "genderism."

But this was not the only objection to the word. Conduct once defended as innocent flirtation, traditional practice, theological doctrine, or "nobody's business" now became easily recognizable as sexist. Naming the abuse would inevitably draw attention to behaviors that many felt were fine just as they were. Struggles over names are rarely without political implications, and the battle over adding "sexism" to the lexicon is a case in point.

Rankism, like sexism and racism, is not a pretty thing. In fact, the adjective "rank" has many meanings, including flagrant, rotten, and fetid. Certainly, rankism is all that and more. Giving it a name that links it linguistically to other disreputable isms makes it easier to spot and harder to defend.

Afflicting primarily those of low rank — those taken for nobodies — rankism takes a wide variety of forms, including maltreatment, discrimination, disrespect, discourtesy, disdain, derision, and condescension. Since the impact of rank-based discrimination is much like that of any other form, it is equally unacceptable.

One accomplishment of the civil rights and women's movements has been to reverse the burden of proof from target to perpetrator. A charge of racism or sexism now puts the accused on the defensive. Likewise, taking up the cause of rankism will put those in positions of power on notice.

The notion of rankism lies at the nexus of morality, civility, and civil rights. By naming and attacking it, we place the goal of human dignity in the context of the battles for civil and women's rights, and breathe new life into all the established identity-based movements.

When people learn that you're writing a book, they often ask what it's about. By trying ideas out on inquisitive friends and strangers, I've learned a great deal. As mentioned earlier, many people are eager to recount how they've been nobodied, even the rich and famous. No matter their current station, they tell their tales with passion, and you've now seen a fair sample of them.

Amidst this enthusiasm, the one objection I sometimes get is to my use of the word "rankism." In the aftermath of the Cold War and turmoil over civil rights, people are wary of anything that sounds like it might be associated with a new movement. "Not another ism," they protest. "Can't you call it something else?"

I've considered many suggestions. But none has proven more apt than "rankism," the merits of which are brevity, rhetorical resonance with the other isms, and explicit incorporation of the word "rank," which describes one's relative position in a hierarchy, thus going to the heart of the matter.

As we've seen, rankism is not so much a new kind of discrimination as it is the common denominator of all the others, the underlying force that gives the familiar ones their capacity to inflict damage. When viewed in this way, virtually all of the isms are seen to be special cases of rankism.

What's more, the familiar isms are but the tip of an iceberg. Below the waterline lies an enormous body of abuses of power sanctioned by both actual and presumed differences in rank. Until rankism is exposed and deprived of legitimacy, we will continue to be plagued by all the otherwise-named forms of discrimination that derive their very lifeblood from it.

Beyond Political Correctness

One reason we blanch at the thought of adding to the list of isms is that we have grown weary of a notion they invariably invoke: political correctness. But it would be a mistake in our battle fatigue to reject the word "rankism," or turn a blind eye to the phenomenon to which it refers. As we come to recognize and rid ourselves of this form of abuse, we deprive all the other isms of their oxygen. And if by political correctness we mean ending the sanction of these isms, then who can validly object? They are indefensible.

What really bothers us about political correctness is not its tenets per se, but that it is used as a weapon. Rather than brandishing it to gain the moral high ground and an edge, we can use its standards instead to remind ourselves of the conditions for a fair society. The principles of political correctness are pointers to social justice much as symmetry principles are criteria for validity in modern physics.

But political correctness is often invoked with an air of self-righteousness and condescension. Such moral rankism causes resentment, especially if the reprimand is for an infraction which is itself rankist. To condemn someone haughtily for rankism is to commit the very offense one is condemning. If moral instruction is to take hold, it must be given in a way that honors the dignity of learner and teacher alike. Delivered with the slightest whiff of patronization, it is doomed to failure. You can't overcome rankism with rankism.

Imagine that you see an adult demeaning a child — for example, picture a soccer mom or dad or a coach humiliating a child for a misplay — and you have an impulse to intervene and protect the child by explaining the damage being done. If an adult poses a threat to a child's health, the urgency of acting swiftly may well outweigh considerations of doing so in a way that would safeguard the dignity of both parties. But it's inherent in the "pass-it-down-the-line" nature of rankism that attempts to stop it will only work if we can find a way to protect the dignity of both perpetrators and victims alike. In the soccer example, that means not insulting the parent or coach as you attempt to shield the child. This principle applies at all levels of behavior — interpersonal, intergroup, and international. In a contest, it does not mean declining to compete; it means competing fairly.

The fact that you can't overcome rankism with rankism explains the puzzling ineffectiveness of many progressive social groups. If a tone of moral superiority pervades an organization and infects its rhetoric, some adherents are attracted because membership affords them an opportunity to feel superior to nonmembers — the "unenlightened." The message being promulgated, no matter how timely and important, will remain unheard and unheeded by the vast majority until, in its content and presentation, it is shorn of moral rankism.

Spiritual leaders and groups, convinced that they are privy to higher knowledge or divine wisdom, share this susceptibility, especially if their doctrine discourages questioning and their behavior cannot be held accountable. Wherever accountability is absent, rankism is apt to take root and grow. The question posed by the Romans, *Quis custodiet ipsos custodes?*

("Who guards the guardians?"), implicitly sounds the warning. Police review boards and ecclesiastical counterparts drawn from the laity provide a remedy.

If rankism were to lose its sanction and rankists found themselves on the defensive, political correctness would be simplified. Its litany of admonitions could then be collapsed into a single rule: safeguard others' dignity as you would your own. As individuals, when we avoid rankism, we automatically avoid interpersonal insults and all the now-discredited isms. As a nation, we become sensitive to signs of hegemonic international behavior.

A Dignitarian Movement

All human beings are born free and equal in dignity and rights.
— United Nations Universal Declaration of Human Rights

An unheralded, unnamed revolution is unfolding in our midst. Everywhere, people are becoming less willing to put up with disrespect. And, like all revolutions, this one is about the distribution of power.

But whereas the civil rights movement was about black empowerment, the women's movement about female empowerment, and the Gray Panthers about senior empowerment, this revolution is about the relative power of *individuals*. It is about interpersonal power. It goes beyond identity groups to include everyone in the human family, with the goal of equal dignity for all in dealings with one another.

The norms that are now shifting are those pertaining to authority. How we get it, and how we use it. Who should have it, and who should not. How people with power should treat those who lack it. Which power-acquiring behaviors are acceptable, and which are not.

We want to see power's credentials. From what does rank derive? What makes status legitimate? What function does hierarchy serve? What are the prerogatives of a title, and where do those prerogatives stop? What is the proper role of height, looks, fame; of connections, know-how, and skill?

Answering these questions requires an investigation of rank, the outer indication of power. It calls for an examination of the difference between uses and abuses of rank. Our subjective experience of dignity or indignity hinges on this critical distinction.

Symptomatic of the shift in attitude toward authority is an unprecedented mistrust of and indifference to electoral politics. Young adults are abandoning it in droves. The reasons are not hard to discern. First, the process is seen as corrupted by campaign contributions, undercutting the one-person, one-vote foundation upon which modern democracy rests. Why bother to vote if the game is fixed?

Second, the political process is not addressing matters that concern people most which, in the absence of war or grave national crises, involve the use and abuse of interpersonal power within our social institutions.

But it is difficult to openly confront issues of rank and power, and we do so only as a last resort. Bringing them up is still considered bad form, and it may well be dangerous. We stand today in relation to rank where we stood two generations ago in relation to race, gender, and sexual orientation. We find the entire subject awkward and embarassing.

The way to overcome our inhibitions about rank is to explore it. We must examine it as it functions among friends and colleagues, and within organizations. We must ask what its proper use is in families, schools, religious institutions, health care organizations, unions, the workplace, and in our nation's international relations.

Sorting out the appropriate role of rank in personal and public life will be as uncomfortable, and as consequential, as has been examining the roles of race and gender. A social revolution pivoting on rank is the next logical step beyond those that have preoccupied us for the last forty years.

The abuse and discrimination still plaguing minorities and women now spring less from the inborn traits that define such groups than from our unconscious and still socially sanctioned impulse to pull rank on one another. In attributing those injustices to color or gender, we are assigning false cause. Pulling rank would continue unabated even if by some miracle we suddenly found all humankind to be of one race, one gender, and one sexual orientation.

The incipient revolution over rank turns out to have nothing to do with rank per se, but rather with abuses of the power differences that correspond to differences in rank. Our successes in distinguishing between race and racism and sex and sexism give us reason to believe we can likewise sort out the differences between rank and rankism. It is not possible to shoo the rhino back into the closet. But by naming rankism and illuminating its effects, we can keep it from fouling our lives.

King for a Day

Don't bow before another person or another nation.
— Mahatma Gandhi (1869–1948)

Indignity signals an abuse of power — or, put the other way round, the abuse of power is incompatible with the principle of inviolate human dignity. Rooting out rankism therefore represents an incremental, programmatic approach toward the establishment of universal human dignity.

Dignity means equal recognition as human beings; but it does not mean equal regard within our specialized capacities as scientists, artists, or athletes. In these areas there are better and worse — winners and losers, if you like. But so what if you fail? You can always get up, dust yourself off, and have another go, your self-respect intact. Or you can change your field. Losing may hurt our pride, but not having a fair chance is an affront to our dignity.

We must learn to acknowledge our strengths (without undue pride), while not feeling shame about our weaknesses. This means being able to say: "Today, I was number one in the 400 meters, but I was terrible at singing." The first performance crowns me "king" of the 400 meters, but only until the next race; the second gets me cut from the choir.

The example of running, pursued to its logical conclusion, is illuminating. Imagine the addition of ever more qualifications (age, height, weight, etc.), thus creating a plethora of more finely differentiated competitive categories, resulting in more and more winners, one in each sliver of a group. If enough factors were considered — medical history, genetic composition, physical and mental condition on the day of the race — then every time anyone ran, he or she would set a world record in the unique specialty defined by that unique set of parameters!

None of these rankings, high or low, has any bearing on our value or dignity as an individual human being. They may bring us fleeting recognition — not less worthy of celebration because of its brevity, but also not related to our fundamental worth. While they may make us "king for a day," that does not make anyone our servant.

And tomorrow, we must always start over. That's the price we pay for eliminating rankism. The gain is that although legitimate rank is always subject to change, everyone is treated with equal respect and guaranteed an equal chance during and following the process. Just as in a foot race, each time around there are no favorites, no presumed winners or losers. This is a far cry from the situation today, in which handicaps abound, favoritism is commonplace, and advantages derived from past rank predetermine future outcomes.

Fame and fortune are often mistaken for the goals of life. In fact, the deepest satisfaction flows from simple recognition from others for whatever we contribute to them. It has nothing to do with trophies, money, or fame, which are prized rather for the protections they afford us against the indignities of this still rankist world.

I knew a man who held AA meetings at his bedside as he lay dying of cancer. He gave of himself until his final days, appreciated by those who sought his counsel. He kept his dignity to the end. Recognition trumps fame. Dignity trumps death.

Chapter Eight

THE ANATOMY OF DISRESPECT

Where do human rights begin? In small places, close to home: the neighborhood; the school or college; the factory, farm or office. Such are the places where every man, woman and child seeks equal justice, equal opportunity, equal dignity without discrimination. Unless these rights have meaning there, they have little meaning anywhere.
—Eleanor Roosevelt (1882–1962)

The Democratization of Authority

Over time, democracies have gradually become more inclusive, widening the franchise to include virtually all adults. Democracy can be seen as *the* great achievement of the nobodies — their transformation from subjects to citizens.

There are signs, however, that all is not well with democracy. Growing voter apathy signals that marginal improvements in our civic institutions are no longer the public's highest priority. Attention is moving away from national government in two opposite directions: closer to home — families, jobs, schools — where the impact of national government is weak, and out into the world. At the global level, actions are now taken unilaterally by governments and agreements made between them which have far-reaching consequences — all without any direct representation on the part of those affected.

The full democratic vision will remain unrealized until its motivating principle — circumscribing rank — is applied to the social institutions that shape our lives on a daily basis. This includes such things as how schools or places of worship are governed, how health care is delivered, and how the enterprises we work for are run.

There are also global policy issues such as international trade, pandemics, and environmental quality on which the people of the world have an extremely indirect say. The emerging world system lacks the democratic mechanisms with which to represent the views of citizens within constituent national democracies. On issues that lie beyond the reach of nation states, individual citizens of these states, even if the states are democracies, have no effective voice. This gives rise to street protests directed at international and supranational organizations such as the World Trade Organization, the World Bank, the International Monetary Fund, and groupings of developed nations like the G8.

History is repeating itself at the global level. Where there are no legitimate channels of expression and no participation in governance, violence occurs. The numerous transnational, nongovernmental organizations that now devote themselves to human rights, trade policy, and the environment are a first step toward the creation of an involved, responsible world citizenry; but clearly, participatory democracy in the global context is in a prenatal stage.

As the fight against the familiar isms has demonstrated, establishing legal protections against the abuse of rank will play an important part in safeguarding human dignity. In our social institutions, traditional legislative remedies must be complemented by regulations and by-laws. These are the locus of the machinery of governance of schools, businesses, and health care systems. Within democracies today, the most disturbing affronts to dignity lie not in the realm of national politics but within these social institutions.

Democratic leaders take care not to insult the citizens who elect them, but schools and HMOs humiliate and demean many of the people they are supposed to serve. Our next task must be to forge agreements that limit use of the power associated with rank, not just in government, but wherever rank signifies authority. In so doing, we can make it clear that the proper role of rank-holders in our social institutions is the same as it is in our civic ones — namely, to serve with the consent of the served. What this means in practice is giving the served a voice and a stake in the governance of these institutions.

The exact form this change will take must be worked out institution by institution, and as with the evolution of civic government, trial and error will be required to find the optimal solution. The best ways of extending the democratic principle into the worlds of business, academia, and health care will likely not be simple replicas of what has worked in civic government. For example, the old formula — one person, one vote — cannot simply be applied without modification in areas where expertise is key. As the problems of designing governance models for these social institutions are solved, there will likely be applications *back* to government that will enable us to improve the quality of service in the civic realm. After all, democracy is not an end in itself, although we sometimes mistake it for such. Rather, the various forms of political democracy are but means — and imperfect ones — for minimizing rankism in civic affairs and protecting our dignity. As such, they are subject to improvement.

As for the governance vacuum that presently exists in the international sphere, nothing resembling an enfranchised world citizenry is yet in the offing. For the present, we must rely on nongovernmental watchdog organizations to speak for us. Exactly how individuals will gain a direct voice in decisions that now affect the entire planet's future (such as on environmental issues, arms, and trade policy) is unforeseeable; but if the evolution of national governments is an indicator, they can be expected to insist on having a say.

There can be many steps involved in redefining a disrespectful relationship, one in which rank is being abused. These range all the way from standing up to a parent, a partner, a teacher, or a boss, to the civil disobedience of liberation movements.

Recognizing the abuse is the first step in defending against it, and that begins when you realize you are in a situation of unequal power in which you are being insulted. Paternalistic relationships may begin as benevolent; but sooner or later, power becomes an issue, and the only way to restore harmony is to distinguish between, and renegotiate, rightful and wrongful uses of rank.

If the circumstance is indeed one of persistent rank abuse, then you have to settle upon a means to combat it. Should you act alone, or join forces with people who are experiencing the same indignities? This will depend critically on whether you can identify others who are facing the same problem. It is also important not to overlook sympathizers among the somebodies — individuals whose high position protects them from rankist abuse, but who are uncomfortable witnessing it. Few revolutions have been carried out without the help of allies from within the dominant group.

If you decide to try to organize support, you have to gain visibility for yourself and your predicament so that potential allies can come forward and stand with you.

From a career civil servant:

> The man in charge of our office during the 1980s — call him HH — used his rank abusively. He had several favorites whom he cultivated — coffee and donuts in his office every morning; long, personal talks during the day — to the disadvantage of the other staff. These lucky few were the ones who advanced, getting the plum assignments.
>
> At some point, HH started an affair with a female secretary. They took trips together, and he promoted her to "professional" ranks even though her work was mediocre. The two of them would travel around together to fun places, not necessarily to where they should have gone to get data for studies.
>
> All of this became offensive to the rest of the staff, particularly the women, and they finally had enough. They ganged up on HH, reported him to Washington, and he was ordered to transfer to a limbo position or leave. The moral is that if higher rank abuses its powers, lower rank can get even by acting collectively. If only one lower-ranked person is involved, it's much harder to resist.

Labor's gains were won by organizing around a common interest — better working conditions — for people who shared a common role. Their tactics anticipate those of a movement against the abuse of rank. Resistance to rankism will likely be organized issue by issue. Any instance wherein the high-ranking are arrogating power to themselves and the low-ranking have no voice or vote in decisions affecting their lives can trigger a protest. As visibility and notoriety build around a specific offense, others suffering similarly, as well as sympathetic witnesses and those who oppose rankism in principle, can add their voices as well. When solidarity with the victims becomes the rule instead of the exception, rankism will have become as taboo as racism and sexism.

The abstract idea of rank abuse cannot be expected to bring about change. Nor can we expect an accusation of rankism to immediately alter people's behavior. But with every successful collective action, old positions involving abuse of power will become harder to defend. At first, charges of rankism will provoke incredulous stares and ritual protestations of innocence. Later, they will call general attention to the practice in question and provide other targets of the same kind of abuse with a rallying point. Eventually, any such complaint will be enough to provoke serious self-examination on the part of the accused.

As the burden of proof shifts from the victims, we shall have to be very careful not to assume that anyone so accused is automatically guilty. A male supervisor:

> What males in positions of authority worry about these days is — "reverse sexism" — being wrongly accused of sexual harassment by a subordinate — because there's simply no way to fight false charges in a knee-jerk, politically correct environment. Power relationships have shifted in recent years, giving subordinates the ability to destroy their superiors. In fact, after having the opposite situation for too long, I think it's now the case that whatever women or minorities complain about is taken to be true, without the need for proof. That is, sexism is assumed of male behavior in general. Men are considered guilty until proven innocent — a reversal of legal presumptions.

It is sobering to realize the extent to which rank permeates our daily lives. In the family, the ranks are parent and child, or kid. In medicine, doctor and patient. In companies, boss and worker, or employer and employee. In elementary schools, teacher and pupil; later on, professor and student. While these "titles" tell us who's in charge, they don't always indicate exactly what they're in charge of or, more pertinently, whether the person in charge holds his or her rank legitimately and exercises it appropriately.

Historically, eliminating rank abuse from government turned subjects into citizens. Parallel transformations will mark the elimination of rank-based abuse in families, health care, employment, and education. I'll first examine these four close-to-home situations, then conclude with an example of organizing against the kind of unchecked exercise of rank that operates in the international realm, where there is as yet no enfranchised citizenry to restrain it.

Family: Kid to Person

Every family has its legends. One of my family's legends is "the spinach standoff."

When I was about four I refused to eat the canned spinach my mother set before me. If you have ever seen a Popeye cartoon, you'll no doubt remember canned spinach. Whenever Popeye faces a crisis that calls for a muscular solution, he opens a can and pours it directly into his upturned mouth. Canned spinach flows like pond scum, which it closely resembles.

My refusal to try even a small spoonful ran up against my mother's Puritan determination that we should all "lick our platters clean." To break the impasse, she issued a threat: "Until you eat the spinach, you get nothing else." I went off to my room determined to hold out for as long as it took. Every few hours my mother would come to the door, open it a few inches, and poke a spoonful of slimy dark spinach through the crack. There is some disagreement in my family about how long the standoff lasted, but no one maintains that it was less than 48 hours. By then the twin pressures of my hunger and my mother's guilt produced a deal: I would open my mouth and permit the spoon laden with scum to enter, but it would be withdrawn without my having to swallow its contents. With this deferential gesture, I won release from captivity and rejoined my parents at the dinner table. Canned spinach was never served again.

The spinach standoff was not about spinach, or even about wasting food. It was about who was boss. It was about the balance of power in the parent-child relationship. On my side, the issue was personal autonomy. On my mother's, it was maintaining parental authority.

The "lick-your-platter-clean" school of dietary discipline was routine in those days. Usually it took the form of "no dessert until your plate is empty." The explanation "because I say so" was regarded as unimpeachable. Military-style obedience — to a parent, teacher, doctor, or employer — was the norm. Rank ruled, right or wrong, no questions asked. The bumper sticker "Question Authority" would not appear until the sixties.

When I was growing up, no public agency would have intervened in a power struggle between parent and child, even one threatening the health of the child; and the spinach standoff did not come close to that. Domestic abuse of all sorts fell under the umbrella of "nobody's business." But imagine a deadlock that goes on for a week, for two weeks. There are times when a parent's authority must be overridden. The difference between proper and improper uses of rank can mean the difference between dignity and indignity, autonomy and servitude or, in extreme cases, life and death.

Over time, in many subtle but telling respects, the way adults treat children has changed. In three generations, we have moved from children being "seen but not heard" to an unimaginable degree of parity between the young and their elders — not parity in knowledge or wisdom, of course, but parity in their status as persons. "Kids are people, too," is the slogan guiding this transformation. Listening to children and considering their views is not the same as indulging them or abdicating parental responsibility for their well-being.

My brothers and I were spanked. Physical domination has always been used to establish who's who, and naturally the practice has figured in child rearing. I unconsciously adopted it with my own first child, became ambivalent with the second, and dropped it entirely with the third and fourth. Today spanking is no more thinkable to me than striking another adult, and I now wonder who I was when I became a parent at twenty-three.

A shift in the balance of power between young and old is fraught with all the apprehension that attends changes in any traditional hierarchy. In this regard, it is reminiscent of the anxieties and fears that have accompanied the empowerment of women and blacks.

The information now available to youth through media and public awareness campaigns exposes them to a broader range of values, viewpoints, and information than ever before. For example, there is heightened awareness of the physical and sexual abuse of children. Teaching the young their rights is a first step in reducing the chance that the power difference between children and adults will be misused.

As the relationships between parents and children evolve, exemplification replaces threat as the primary motivational mechanism. Good parents have always known that being a worthy example invites emulation and gets more lasting results than does ridicule, humiliation, or punishment.

A college math major writes:

> When I was in elementary school, I had a friend whose parents were very reluctant to give reasons for their decisions. "Because I said so," "Because you're not old enough," and "Because life isn't fair" were their justifications for everything. Sometimes they would change the subject or ignore their daughter altogether. I distinctly remember at age nine being disturbed by this and most of all, being afraid to approach my friend's parents with questions, or even just in conversation, for fear of being treated like a three-year-old. I was always thankful to go home, where I felt comfortable and could get good information about anything I wanted.
>
> About a year ago, I visited a different friend of mine (then 20 years old) and noticed that her mother avoids having adult conversations with her. The mother tries desperately to regain the authority she has lost and when this fails, abuses what authority she has left. This is an example of the embarrassing power struggles that can result from 20 years of treating children like nobodies once they grow up and realize they are not.
>
> There is nothing I am more thankful for than the supportive, respectful parents I have. They make me want to give these same things to others.

Baby-boomer child-rearing practices represent a sea change in the parent-child hierarchy. Many boomers were raised on the outdated verities that crumbled in the wake of the social protests that marked the sixties of their youth. Consequently, they were less doctrinaire in their views, more open to engaging in a give-and-take with their own children. Their legacy as parents is to have raised a generation of young people who have experienced unprecedented personal dignity while growing up. Today's youth are accustomed to being listened to and, accordingly, are good candidates for taking a principled stand against the abuse of rank. One wonders if their parents will be as deaf to their arguments in support of this new cause as their grandparents were blind to the injustice of segregation and the crippling effects of the feminine mystique. It took the likes of Bull Conner and his police dogs to remove the nation's blinders to the evils of Jim Crow. What will it take to open peoples' eyes to the pervasiveness and corrosiveness of rankism?

We should not be surprised if the recognition that "kids are people, too" eventually leads to pressure to lower the voting age below 18. Today many teens are better informed than their elders, yet they are taxed without representation. The question naturally arises as to why the needs of the most vulnerable among us — young children and adolescents — are given no weight in electoral politics, which affects their lives so critically.

Obviously, for young children, the notion of casting one's own vote would be absurd. A reasonable mechanism for giving electoral weight to the interests of the young would have to be thoughtfully designed. But this would not be an insuperable obstacle if the task were to be embraced philosophically. Given the aging of the population, failure to give electoral weight to the interests of the young will result, very soon, in disproportionate power for the elderly. It's a recipe for national ossification.

Health: Patient to Client

As mentioned earlier, a partnership between medical professionals and their clients is taking shape as more people take responsibility for their health and view their doctors not as gods, but rather as expert consultants.

Health insurance companies and health maintenance organizations (HMOs) introduce a new layer of complexity into the equation. These corporate entities enjoy a tremendous power advantage over the people they serve because their customers cannot easily take their business elsewhere. The power imbalance is compounded by the fact that health information, by its very nature, is technical, ambiguous, and consequential in the extreme.

It is ironic that as relationships with doctors are becoming less rank-conscious, patients are experiencing a loss of power in their dealings with health care organizations. And doctors, who have had to accommodate themselves to growing sophistication of their patients, find themselves subordinated to financial managers charged with containing medical expenditures. The result is that although doctors and patients feel more like peers to each other, they both feel like nobodies vis-à-vis those who manage health care.

It is not part of this book's purpose to propose an answer to the health care crisis. But one thing is clear. Any solution that does not address the issues of rank that pervade the system will be short-lived. If the process itself of designing the next generation of social institutions eschews paternalism and includes the voices and votes of those to be served, the businesses, HMOs, and schools of the future are much more likely to be cleansed of rank abuse.

Work: Employee to Partner

A quiet anti-authoritarian revolution is gaining momentum in the world of business as it becomes apparent that management that does not respect the dignity of workers is counterproductive in knowledge-based enterprises. Businesses now need creative and self-motivated employees. Command and control may work for an assembly line, but it severely handicaps information-driven enterprises.

Individuals tend to hold reserves of energy in check until they see how to use it to their own highest interest. The challenge is to release more of that energy. One thing firms can do is make sure that all employees see better futures ahead of them. There's little room at the top if managers and executives hang on to their positions forever. Unless *they* have ways to move up and out, there is nowhere for junior employees to go. Here is how the workplace of the future might look.

Rank would be awarded and held in the context of a particular task. Recognition would be given upon the completion of that task. Afterwards, new tasks would bring possibilities for new ranks, with the constant flux of opportunity fostering a spirit of cooperation rather than competition. The correlation between decision-making and salary would also be reexamined. Asking a good question — one that spares the firm the consequences of a bad decision — would be rewarded as much as making a good decision.

Firms would incorporate into their business plans scenarios for advancement. To retain the loyalty of their co-workers, executives would show no favoritism to somebodies and take great care not to abridge the privileges and immunities of nobodies. The spirit of the Fourteenth Amendment, with its guarantee of "equal protection," would apply to employment as it does to citizenship. Companies would take pride in being places where everyone experienced equal dignity, had equal opportunity, and received equal justice.

Good business practice holds many lessons for educational reform. But by their very nature, schools have got one thing right: students don't stay around until retirement or death — they graduate and move on. In the labor environment of the future, workers will be seen less as employees holding down a job and more as students learning and progressing from level to level. To create room at the top so others have a chance for upward mobility, resources must be devoted to "graduating" executives. Personnel officers will assume responsibility for seeing that everyone in the firm has somewhere to go, whether inside or outside the company, and will assist them in doing so.

George Washington was right. When people feel they are working for themselves, productivity improves. In the future, the "mailroom-to-boardroom" story will become less exceptional; employee co-owners, with a share of the equity, more common; and the income and other gaps between the highest and lowest paid will narrow.

Environmental consciousness seemed irrelevant to the bottom line until businesses realized that their stand on the subject mattered to the public. Similarly, the goal of reducing rank abuse in the workplace may seem at first to be a distraction and a nuisance. But as success in engaging workers' self-interest shows up as profit, hierarchical management structures will flatten, question-asking will be more rewarded, and decision-making roles will be assigned on a task-by-task basis.

Since rankism is an indicator of dysfunction, detecting it is a vital responsibility of leadership. Great leaders instinctively set an example that militates against it. They neither abuse their own rank, nor tolerate such abuses among their subordinates. Their actions — from Joan of Arc to Shakespeare's Henry V to George Washington — set an example that inspires the troops.

The Enron Example

The Enron story brings to mind those old engravings that show pickpockets working a crowd of Londoners gathered to witness the hanging of a pickpocket. In the world of business, it is still common for people of high rank to use their power to exploit those lower on the ladder. At Enron, top executives and other insiders lined their pockets at the expense of employees, shareholders, and the public.

In the business world more generally, executives and board members award themselves salaries thousands of times those paid to their employees while shielding their retirement savings from downside risk. The victims of corporate corruption become targets for no reason other than that they are weak and vulnerable — that is, because of their low rank.

Like racism and sexism, corruption is a betrayal of democratic ideals and, like them, it poses a mortal threat to democracy. The Enron example shows that rooting out the kind of unfairness that issues from corruption requires rooting out rankism.

Although we are hypersensitive to the injustices that befall us as individuals, we are slow to organize against those that affect us all. In the aftermath of the big corporate scandals, public perception is that people of high rank in powerful positions don't feel accountable to ordinary people and can aggrandize themselves with impunity.

But experience suggests that overcoming the inequity resulting from such corruption is within our power. Remedies such as strengthening regulatory agencies and reforming accounting practices and campaign finance, as critical as those are, will not be enough. The change required is comparable in magnitude to the transformations America has undergone to address other great historic injustices.

Once we have identified a misuse of power and given it a name, we have repeatedly succeeded in shifting abusers to the defensive and then reducing their numbers, often to the vanishing point. We have overthrown kings and tyrants and placed political power in the hands of the people. We have reined in monopolies with antitrust legislation. We have limited the power of bosses through unionization. And we can do the same with rankism.

As this happens, the business environment will become increasingly inhospitable to Enron-like corruption, much as America has, over time, become less tolerant of discrimination against all the various identity groups.

Learning: Student to Learner

In knowledge-based societies, the right to learning becomes paramount. Education is ripe for a democratizing revolution, and nothing will do more to improve the quality of our educational institutions than clarifying the role of rank within them.

A fundamental goal consistent with collective economic health and individual fulfillment is first-class, lifelong education, equally available to all. Common decency and human dignity demand that no one be denied a realistic chance to start well in life, or to start over.

The three pillars on which education has traditionally rested — requirements, faculty tenure, and the nonrepresentation of learners in governance — must each be remolded if students are to commit themselves, heart and soul, to their own education and transform themselves from students into learners.

Requirements

After a year of heated argument, the Oberlin faculty, in 1971, voted by a narrow margin to abolish general course requirements. Only within the major were there certain courses that students were obliged to take, ensuring at least a taste of in-depth learning.

Under the old system, two thousand students were being forced to take physical education. Once the requirement was lifted and they were free to choose, just a handful signed up. Quite a drop! But, that's not the end of the story; it's merely an indication of how much students hated the mandatory program.

Fearing the college would eliminate the entire department for lack of enrollments, the physical education faculty redesigned its program from top to bottom. They introduced courses they had resisted for years — martial arts, dance, trampoline, the history and sociology of sports — and they changed their attitudes toward students. The department had been run like boot camp as long as the supply of captive recruits lasted. Removing the requirement instantly instilled the service ethic that we take for granted in commercial enterprises. Within two years, enrollments were at pre-abolition levels. The atmosphere was radically changed, the department transformed and reinvigorated.

With the abolition of general requirements, the language departments also became vulnerable to mass desertion. As a result, for the first time in their lives, professors had to make their classes interesting to students, or lose them and jeopardize their jobs. To that degree, they became accountable to the students.

Within a year, a good part of the college's entire liberal arts curriculum had been reworked and rejuvenated. New courses and majors appeared in the catalogue. There were new programs for study abroad. Interdisciplinary collaborations blossomed. The act of signing up for a course became a voluntary expression of interest in the subject.

Faculty members who opposed this reform had argued that we'd be turning the college into a "candy store." They feared we'd be indulging the students, graduating some who were entirely ignorant of math or a foreign language, or some other subject "with which every educated person should be acquainted."

In practice, however, although students now made the final decisions about what courses they took, they did so only after availing themselves of much good guidance and advice. Once they realized their future was in their own hands, they sought the counsel of teachers they most admired and trusted, weighed it very seriously, and more often than not, they followed it. If there was in the end a narrowing of the range of courses chosen, it was barely detectable.

Choosing one's educational path is in a way like choosing one's lovers: it's better that we do it ourselves because even though we may err, we learn much more from our own mistakes than from the results of decisions made for us by others. Young people who feel secure in their right to make critical choices for themselves are much more apt to consult with their mentors.

The most schooling can hope to do, given the exponential explosion of knowledge, is to instill a lifelong passion for learning. It is most likely to do so if students are encouraged to pursue and develop their own interests. There is no greater success for an educational institution than to have its graduates leave more enthusiastic about learning than they were when they arrived.

Tenure

In education the only issue touchier than requirements is tenure. Tenure gives teachers lifetime professional security, independent of on-the-job performance. Whereas once it provided academic freedom for vulnerable professors and teachers, now it perpetuates the entrenched power of the strong. Tenure is like the divine right of kings — an outdated sacrosanct privilege of a few somebodies held at the expense of many nobodies. Rather than protecting the pursuit of excellence, it undercuts the principle that rank, to warrant continuing respect, must be periodically re-earned.

The fact that many teachers are true to their vocations, never lose their love for learning and teaching, and embody the very heart and soul of education does not alter the case against tenure. Such teachers would be just as good without it, and don't need it to protect their jobs.

The preponderance of tenure in the upper ranks makes it an important factor in pricing higher education beyond the means of many, because the average pay for senior teachers is considerably more than that for their juniors. Tenure is all the more insupportable because many new Ph.D.s would bring more enthusiasm and better training to their teaching than a large number of the professors who now have a lock on the best positions.

In any other area of human endeavor we would ask, "How can we cut costs and keep our customers?" Once educators put their minds to this problem, they will come up with creative solutions that are both humane and academically sound. They should not be asked to give up the job security that tenure provides except as part of a fundamental restructuring of the entire educational enterprise. Varied opportunities for teachers to become new somebodies must be just as available as opportunities for students upon graduation. Only then could the profession reasonably be expected to relax its claims to the security afforded by tenure.

Governance

When the focus was on political justice, citizens demanded the vote and took responsibility for governance. Learners can be expected to take parallel action in the coming century, as awareness grows that nothing affects a person's chances of achieving human fulfillment more than education.

Such predictions are not mere speculation. The last round of significant educational reform was contemporaneous with the demands of college students that they be recognized as adults. In the United States, as it became clear that we could not send eighteen-year-olds to fight the war in Vietnam while denying them suffrage, the voting age was lowered from twenty-one to eighteen by constitutional amendment. During this same period, college students began criticizing their schools for assuming the role of surrogate parents. They insisted that they themselves, not administrators or teachers, be allowed to make their own personal and, increasingly, educational decisions.

During the first week of my presidency at Oberlin, a student with hair down to his shoulders walked into my office complaining that the baseball coach would not let him play for the college unless he got a haircut. In the course of our conversation, he told me he had hit .550 the previous season. In a school not known for athletics, this kid was a Samson. I suspected his prowess might give me some leverage with the coach.

I dropped in on him later that day. He admitted that he needed the slugger's bat in the line-up, but took the position that he'd rather do without him than look as though he were losing control of the team. His logic — equating hair length with discipline — reminded me of why I had hated the physical education classes I'd been required to take in that very gymnasium fifteen years earlier.

We quickly reached an impasse, and I asked the coach if he could think of any way out. To my astonishment, he said, "Just order me to let him play, and I will." He wanted me to overrule him so he could win some games without looking as though he had given in to student pressure.

The coach saw the problem in terms of rank: since as president mine was higher than his, there was no disgrace in giving in to me; in fact, it would be in the line of duty. The important thing was to preserve the hierarchy, and an order from me would leave the command structure intact. I would play a somebody to him, and he would remain a somebody to his players.

Against some deep instinct that such a compromise was not in the students' best long-term interests, but wishing to get the matter behind me, I agreed. The coach maintained his pride and authority and Samson, with hair unshorn and *his* dignity intact, played ball and won the league batting title that year.

This story speaks to the limits of the reach of all the various movements against the isms. They have never gotten to the deeper root of the matter, which has to do with rank and power. The various liberation movements have lopped a few heads off the Hydra, but left the monster alive to continue its predations in interpersonal relations, business, the trades and professions, and the schools.

In the end, Samson — a nobody — was permitted to play baseball for Oberlin. That he was one of 3000 students whose tuition kept the college in business, but who had no say in its governance, did not enter the discussion. We somebodies paternalistically made all the significant decisions, and our traditional right to do so went largely unquestioned.

Under intense student pressure during a four-year period from the late sixties into the early seventies, America's colleges and universities updated virtually every aspect of their operations. In France also, in the demonstrations of May 1968, students demanded that the Sorbonne reform its age-old curriculum. But with a few notable exceptions, students did not insist upon assuming a significant role in the governing of their schools. When the dust settled, institutional decision-making was still as it had been before the whirlwind of reforms.

It was during this time that Switzerland was reconsidering its centuries-old policy of the exclusively male franchise. To no one's surprise, Swiss men at first decided that it was in the national interest that they, and only they, do the voting. Though administrators and faculties everywhere deplored this chauvinism, when it came to sharing power within their own institutions, they too decided it was in everyone's best interest that they remain in charge.

So campus unrest, which had its origins in paternalism, ended by leaving the paternalistic system of governance in place. The only difference was that the particular issues that had sparked the unrest were resolved, stilling the voices of protest for a time. Swiss men have since seen the light and extended the franchise to women, but for the most part, educators continue to cling to their monopoly on power.

As gatekeepers to the future, teachers have exercised an awesome influence on whether their pupils grow up to be somebodies or nobodies. Given the centrality of education in knowledge-based societies, democracy's next step depends on nothing so much as on students assuming responsibility for it themselves, along with commensurate authority. In the end, learners will honor teachers not for their superior power, but for their superior knowledge; not as taskmasters, but as exemplars.

Engaging Learners as Allies

Mentors provide inspirational leadership without the hierarchical differentiation of master and student.
— John A. Wheeler, American physicist (1911–)

Nothing seems to bring about fundamental political or educational reform except insistence on fuller personhood — by citizens and learners, respectively — and the assumption of self-responsibility this entails. The fact that more and more college students in the coming years will be middle-aged adults retraining themselves for new careers makes ridding education of paternalism both more urgent and more feasible. An interesting development in this regard is the growth of remote learning via the Internet, in which face-to-face contact with teachers is no longer involved. Innovations such as this will likely contribute to the breakdown of traditional academic hierarchies.

Removing the rank abuse that pervades elementary and secondary school education — much of it among peers — will be more challenging, but the trend in that direction is already visible. Charter schools have achieved a measure of self-governance, freeing teachers from bureaucratic rules so they can focus on the needs of their pupils. The next step is to find ways to involve learners along with their teachers in the process of governing.

As the information age made authoritarian regimes and their associated command economics untenable, so the advent of knowledge-based societies will make command education obsolete as well. We simply will not be able to carry out our most important task — education — without effecting in it, too, an equivalent democratic shift: making students into partners.

Introducing market forces and participatory democracy into education is an even more daunting challenge than converting communist autocracies to free market democracies. At least the communist world had the United States and Western Europe to look to as models, albeit imperfect ones. In the realm of education, no proven alternatives exist, and new ones cannot be invented and tested overnight.

Reckless reforms such as eliminating ranking altogether, lowering standards in the name of building self-esteem, or putting students completely in charge of schools will not work. What *could* work would be to judge reforms according to whether or not they contributed to making learners into allies in the business of their own education. If this were the standard used, then transformation could evolve systematically, guided by empirical results. Until that happens, we should not be surprised that students subjected to command education behave like workers in a command economy; most do just enough to get by.

Much experimentation will be required to infuse the principles of democracy into learning. We can start by listening to what learners want, instead of just telling them what they have to do. Their first responses may very well not be the answer, but they should be evaluated on an equal footing with other suggestions.

The current monolithic organization of education hamstrings a trial-and-error search for better alternatives. Faced with stagnation and failure of the present magnitude, the answer is not another round of incremental change within the old framework. Most such reforms — whether progressive or conservative — disappoint because after the novelty wears off, the overall level of student motivation declines to previous levels. Instead, a new framework must be designed that encourages initiative and innovation, empowers students, increases their involvement and satisfaction, and rewards productivity gains.

If we've come to understand anything about learning, it's that people's interests and cognitive styles vary enormously. As learners and teachers both find responsible and creative roles in its governance, education will rapidly evolve individualized pathways that will carry millions of apathetic students, and many of their frustrated teachers, out of Nobodyland.

When rank reflects excellence, coercion is not needed. People who are seeking their own fulfillment do so with an energy and commitment that dwarfs any that could be commandeered, whether in the state, the family, the workplace, or the school.

There is no magic "fix" for the ills of education. So long as students must surrender a piece of their dignity to the current system, many will continue to withhold a significant part of themselves from the process of learning. Societies that uproot rankism in their schools will lead the world in the twenty-first century, as those that curtailed it in government led in the twentieth.

A Better Game than War: Ciphers to Citizens

So long as anti-militarists propose no…moral equivalent of war…they fail to realize the full inwardness of the situation.
— William James, American philosopher and psychologist (1842–1910)

Thus far, we have focused on rank abuse as it occurs between individuals and within institutions. Rankism also arises — often with serious consequences — between groups. For example, a corporate monopoly may use its financial clout to put a company that poses a competitive threat out of business. Antitrust legislation was designed to prevent this abuse of power. Of course, the judgment as to whether a given company is violating the law or whether it is simply engaging in fair competition in the pursuit of high rank and its just rewards is often arguable and may have to be settled in the courts.

Of even greater consequence than corporate battles are those between nation states. When one of them pulls rank on another, demanding subservience or surrender, the result is either capitulation or war.

History is replete with examples of groups attempting to wrest recognition from one another. Wars of aggression are usually an assertion of primacy tied to tribal or national identity. In their quest for recognition on the world stage, some nations have won glory. Often, however, it proved to be a passing glory, even a prelude to catastrophe.

A humiliated people may heed the call of a demagogic leader in order to avenge and redeem itself by establishing a new, attractive identity at the expense of its neighbors. One Nazi SS officer, reminiscing about German military victories in the early years of World War II, remarked: "It was with unrivaled pride that we saw the world. We were somebody." As it turned out, just a few years later, the "thousand-year Reich" lay in ashes.

War can also be undertaken to slough off a stagnant identity in a kind of tacit collective suicide. Laurens Van der Post, who spent World War II in a Japanese prison, wrote of his captors, "The war was...an instinctive search for renewal by destroying a past they could not escape except through the disaster of utter collective defeat."

Whatever its genesis, war between sovereign states has grave repercussions for statesmen and citizens alike. During World War I, the French Prime Minister Clemenceau said, "War is much too serious a matter to be entrusted to the military." In this famous pronouncement, he was in fact laying his own claim to ultimate authority over war policy. He was attempting to limit the role of ranking officers in military decisions. Subordination of military to civilian authority is a landmark in the struggle to circumscribe the scope of rank.

During the Cold War, the Bomb made nobodies of everybody. As a consequence, questions of war and peace became everybody's business, not just that of the politicians. Foreign affairs became too important to be left to professional diplomats, and another Clemenceau-like shifting of responsibility was called for. We nobodies had to get into the game, welcome or not. The commoners of the world — business people, travelers, tourists, students — had to go out and create, through personal relationships with their overseas counterparts, a post-Cold War context and climate that would persuade government officials on both sides that arms limitation was feasible and prudent.

As the nuclear arms race intensified, thousands of ordinary people on both sides of the Iron Curtain became involved in this endeavor. Gaining the name "citizen diplomacy," it marked the beginnings of a global citizenry wherein nobodies stopped ceding responsibility for world affairs to a de facto transnational oligarchy and instead took it upon themselves. In the spirit of Clemenceau's remark, their credo was, "War is much too serious to be entrusted to statesmen."

Unaffiliated, globally disenfranchised citizens now have a powerful new organizing tool in the Internet, but in the dark days of the Cold War, you pretty much had to go there in person if you wanted to interact with individuals of the Soviet Union. In 1968, I made such a visit to Moscow and Leningrad, and like all visitors in those days, was shepherded around by an Intourist guide. Her answers to my questions were not reassuring. For example, to one about how mental illness was treated in Soviet society, she replied, "There is no mental illness under communism. Mental illness is a by-product of capitalism." Yet everyone knew at the time that dissenters were incarcerated in psychiatric hospitals.

After many such experiences in which the realities of myself and my hosts seemed to differ so radically, the words of the Russian writer Alexander Solzhenitsyn came to mind: "If decade after decade the truth cannot be told, ... one's fellow countrymen become harder to understand than Martians." Indeed, the question that stuck in my mind after this trip was, "Are the Russians Martians?"

During the Cold War, I traveled frequently to the Soviet Union, twice taking the Trans-Siberian railway across the country with my family, and the "Martian question" continued to haunt me. It took more than a decade for me to answer it to my satisfaction.

Stereotyping others is incompatible with according them equal dignity. Stereotypes are the enemy of respect and recognition. When Cold War citizen diplomats from both sides of the Iron Curtain got to know each other as individuals, the mutual stereotyping that helped sustain the conflict began to crumble.

In retrospect, I see this kind of citizen diplomacy as a kind of performance art, in which our personal presence gave testimony to the fact that the lives of real people were at stake. Taking my wife and one-year-old to a talk I gave at the Institute for the Study of the USA and Canada did more to convey this to my Soviet hosts than anything I said in my speech.

Performance art and political activism are actually close cousins. Rosa Parks, in the role of civil rights activist, triggered a bus boycott in Montgomery, Alabama; the dramatic impact of her protest stirred the civil rights movement nationwide. A few years later Tommie Smith and John Carlos, by raising their gloved fists in the black power salute on the victory stand at the Mexico City Olympics, signaled the end of black obeisance to the world. To some, their gesture was outrageous insubordination — to others, an echo of the "Don't Tread On Me" emblazoned on the first official American flag in 1775. In the same spirit, one of the most enduring images of the twentieth century was the anonymous man in a white shirt with shopping bags facing down a tank in Tiananmen Square in Beijing in 1989. Such dramatic actions against the abuse of rank leave indelible marks on our collective psyche, and play a crucial part in precipitating and consolidating psycho-tectonic shifts.

Performance art makes the invisible visible. Invisible, you're a nobody; visible, you can stand for a cause that others will join. Visibility is the first step toward mutual recognition and equality of dignity. These assuage the recognition disorder that, left untreated, poses the threat of violence, even war.

Citizen diplomacy is oversimplified if it's seen only as a quest for peace. To those who live with injustice, peace means a continuation of their suffering. Rather than make peace a goal in itself, citizen diplomats in the U.S. and their counterparts in Europe and the USSR aimed to make war unattractive and unnecessary. They offered another way to get what warmongers have always promised — recognition, respect, and dignity. You can't put war out of business with peace alone; after a while, that will prove boring and the war party will regain its hold. But you *can* displace war by offering people a "better game." That game is the activist one of mutual recognition.

It turns out that what people need and want is not to dominate others, but to be recognized by them. Recognition is not in finite supply; it's unlimited. The getting-to-know-you game is not a zero-sum game — that is, one in which your loss equals my gain, and vice versa. Rather it's what is known in mathematics as a non-zero-sum game — one in which *both* players can end up better off than they began. Recognizing another person or another nation does not reduce the recognition they give you. The end of the Cold War brought recognition to both sides. Recognizing the Russians did not diminish Americans.

It took a decade — one during which I lost my somebody status and experienced being a nobody — for me to connect the dots. They led from the humiliations I witnessed and experienced as a child in the classroom, to the identity-based movements of the sixties, to the realization that in the Cold War nuclear standoff, until we took diplomacy into our own hands, we the people were not citizens — we were ciphers. When the pieces of the puzzle finally came together, they took the form of a face, an arrogant condescending face — the face of rankism.

The late twentieth century is likely to appear in retrospect as the point at which the pursuit of national aggrandizement by violent means lost its sanction. While this reversal in attitude has not yet seen the end of war, in the aftermath of the Cold War the onus of justification is now on would-be aggressors. With every passing decade, war between nations becomes a less defensible option.

One word of caution is in order. It is in the nature of contests for rank and recognition that either side can unilaterally choose to ignore the rules, and may be tempted to do so if it thinks it can get away with it. This means we need always be ready to meet such opponents — whether a nation threatening war, a group threatening terrorism, or an individual threatening crime — in a cruder form of contest. At the same time, we should welcome potential adversaries wanting to engage in more evolved, less violent forms of competition.

With the passage of enough time, reversion to brute force will become less likely, but never impossible. To keep this option from being too tempting, a superior power willing and able to dominate rule-breakers must be kept in readiness and in sight — as police are used to discourage crime, and armed forces to deter attack.

The best way to prevent violence, however, is to make the new game attractive, fair, and open to all players. The more this is done, the more demagogic appeals for primitive aggression will fall on deaf ears, and the more relapses into crime, terrorism, and war will diminish, perhaps to the vanishing point.

People give up power voluntarily only to grasp greater power. People abandon a familiar game only to take up a better one. With the advent of weapons of mass destruction, the anvil of war has become less and less available for forging national identities. The game of international recognition that is taking shape in the post-Cold War era is indeed a better game than war. Recognition remains a primary motivation, but the recognition sought is mutual, among peers, not the obeisance paid by the vanquished to a victor. Compared to this new game, the old one looks like a bloodthirsty pirate tale; compared to dialogues now developing, the propaganda of the past sounds like the braggadocio of adolescents. As the English poet William Cowper (1731–1800) wrote:

> But war's a game, which,
> Were their subjects wise,
> Kings would not play at.

National Security in the Twenty-First Century

In the aftermath of the September 11th terrorist attacks, sympathizers filled the streets in third world cities. Their demonstrations are reminiscent of civil rights protests in America in the 1960s.

Then, African-Americans were on the march. Campuses seethed, violence mounted, cities were torched. At first, agitators were depicted as malcontents and hooligans; their leaders were characterized as madmen and evildoers. But as millions of Americans watched on television, it soon became clear that in addition to the vast majority of black Americans, a growing number of whites sympathized with their cause.

Confronted with a grave threat to national unity, Americans realized that the problem lay not with the demonstrators, but rather with the racism that fueled their outrage. What the vast majority of African-Americans wanted was not, as some charged, to substitute black rule for white. Neither was it to set up their own separate state. They simply wanted to end second-class citizenship and to have a fair chance at the American dream.

Within a decade, a number of fundamental policy changes had been made. The administration of law and order was integrated; job discrimination was outlawed; segregation of public facilities was ended; the number of minority students in higher education was increased tenfold, thus providing entrée to the professions. Discrimination in housing became illegal; voting rights were guaranteed. Attitudinal changes accompanied the political. By the 1970s, it had become an impediment to career advancement to be known as a racist.

In the end, a half-dozen major changes sufficed to pry open doors that had long been closed to African-Americans. Once Americans opted for inclusion, the protests subsided. Demagogues of both the left and the right — black radicals and white extremists — lost their audience and their influence. Two generations later, racism, which long enjoyed the support of the silent majority, is in disrepute.

The terrorists who target America do not lack for sympathizers. That they live in Jakarta, Karachi, Damascus, and Cairo provides small comfort in a world shrunk by technology and ease of travel.

This time the cause of popular unrest is not racial injustice. Nor, despite the fact that the marchers are primarily Muslims, is it religion. Ironically, America stands for religious tolerance, while the protesters and their leaders champion religious conformity.

Differences notwithstanding, there is one unmistakable parallel between the demonstrations of the sixties and those around the world today: the majority of the participants are disenfranchised and dispossessed. They resent the lack of opportunity to make something of themselves, and hold America responsible for their predicament.

Whether we are at fault for disillusionment in the third world is arguable. What is not in dispute is that the lives of millions of young people in these regions are going to waste. Protesters are trying to tell us this in the only way they can. If their desperation does not elicit our sympathy, it should at least alert us to danger, because for the young, the step from desperation to desperado is a short one.

America has long been regarded everywhere as a land of opportunity. With the end of the Cold War, it also became the one and only superpower. As third world youth feel their lives slipping away, it's understandable that they hold accountable the nation they see as all-powerful, and that their initial admiration turns quickly to disappointment and then hate.

To help the dispossessed achieve meaningful lives, we have to find a way to do internationally what we did domestically in the 1960s. Facing increasingly violent civil rights protests, we identified and eliminated racial barriers to opportunity and participation. As despair lifted, militancy subsided. Opportunity worked then, and it will work again. Opportunity is all that ever works.

Second only to the need for food and shelter, people crave a chance to contribute, and to gain recognition for their contributions. As part of a commitment to realizing this goal universally, why not subject our foreign policies to a simple test: do they further equal opportunity both at home *and abroad*? Nothing would serve our long-range interests more than helping the citizens of developing nations throw off futility and despair. Nothing less will end the appeal of demagogues who preach violence, often for their own purposes. We can only stop the threat of terrorism by lifting the gloom which predisposes people to support it.

Barriers to equal opportunity take the form of rankism. Put the other way around, a recipe for creating opportunity worldwide is to identify and eliminate abuses of rank. This will not be easy, but it is possible. For us to regain a sense of security, it is now also necessary.

When a few can terrorize a superpower, a good offense is no longer an adequate defense. It becomes equally important to avoid giving offense. This does not mean ingratiating ourselves with others or condoning violence; but it does mean scrupulously respecting their dignity and adopting policies that promote opportunity for them as well as ourselves.

As mounting civil disobedience in the sixties brought home the political and social costs of racism, so does terrorism now announce the cost of rankism. Nothing can justify the September 11th attacks on the World Trade Center and the Pentagon. Terrorism is an arrogation of power so horrific that, to justify their deeds, perpetrators feel they must represent themselves as doing God's work. Closer examination usually reveals that the leaders of terrorist movements harbor personal political ambitions in their countries of origin. Faced with such deceit and hubris, we have no choice but to do what we can to identify and incapacitate known offenders, in hopes of preventing future attacks. It was likewise necessary to pursue the arsonists who put the torch to Detroit and Los Angeles in the sixties.

But law enforcement and counterintelligence constitute only half a policy — the defensive half. While actively pursuing terrorists, Western governments must also become pro-active by working to alleviate the futility and suffering of life in the world's poorest nations.

No people has ever been willing to compromise its dignity, except as a temporizing tactic. Dignity is sacrosanct, and when it is abrogated, there is a heavy price to pay. As we have seen, indignity in the family stunts personal growth; in the schools, it sabotages learning; on the job, it taxes productivity. Likewise, in international relations, indignity threatens peace and undercuts development and global prosperity.

While a specific act of terror has many complex causes, there can be little doubt that international rankism is one of the factors that creates a political climate hospitable to those who commit it. Modern technology, which creates weapons of mass destruction and places them within the reach of many, now makes the price of international rankism prohibitive.

How to Win Respect and Safeguard Dignity

This section explores what individuals can do to win respect and safeguard their dignity without insulting that of others. Rather than generalize, I am going to let seven individuals describe their encounters with rankism and tell in their own words what they did to defend themselves or others against it.

The managing editor of a national business magazine writes:

> Aida cleans my house, and has become my friend. To make ends meet, she also teaches high school science and has a job one night a week in a nursing home. She is from the Philippines, one of the working poor we hear so much about.
>
> Aida has been having trouble with her left knee — a lot of pain walking. Her very inferior HMO had her lined up for surgery, but something about this bothered both of us. The hospital was lousy, the facts didn't add up. So my friend Joan (Aida cleans her house, too) and I found a knee specialist and treated Aida to a second opinion. I went with her to her appointment.
>
> The doctor decided to recommend a physical therapist, and wanted to know what geographic location would suit Aida. She was so unaccustomed to speaking up, to feeling she was on an equal level with a medical professional, that at first she couldn't even tell him, "No, Bayside is not convenient; do you know someone in Forrest Hills?" That was the role I filled, communicating on a peer basis with the doctor.
>
> But by the end of the appointment, Aida had actually started to ask questions on her own! This man was an excellent physician, not at all condescending, and the rankism involved here was that which Aida had internalized from previous demeaning experiences. So as it turned out, we left the office and a half-block away, she thought of another question, went back without me, and asked it herself. This may not sound like much, but it was a very big deal to Aida.

From a ninety-year-old advocate for seniors comes this story of grassroots democracy as an antidote to bureaucratic autocracy:

> In the 1950s, the Port of New York Authority, which is all-powerful in New York and New Jersey, decided that another international airport was needed to serve New York City. The

site they chose was known as "The Great Swamp," an area of about 25 square miles, the headwaters of the Passaic River in rural New Jersey. One part of it came within two miles of my home and a mile of the new school my children were attending. With a runway just one mile away, the noise level would have interfered with schoolwork.

The Great Swamp had blueberries growing in it. I could pick a ten-quart pail there in an hour. It also was a wonderful place for kids to go camping. Deer and other wildlife roamed about.

The townsfolk were angry and as citizens, we took action. We organized a march on the capitol in Trenton, and traipsed into the chamber where the governor was giving a speech with a banner that read, "Save our Swamp!"

Shortly afterwards, lawyers who lived in town found out who the owners of the swamplands were and quietly bought up the property. Our congressional representative collected the deeds to the land and, in our name, made a gift of them to the federal government for a wildlife preserve.

No airport was built in our town. We defeated the mighty Port Authority. Instead, Newark Airport was enlarged and today blueberries still grow and deer still live in New Jersey's Great Swamp.

From a woman of 55 who's employed as a temp at a medical research institution:

> In the organization I work for, the hierarchy starts in the tunnels under the buildings, where blacks and Hispanics labor in the trades that maintain the physical plant. On the top of the ladder — the 11th floor — obsequious secretaries serve the top-brass MDs as if they were gods on Mt. Olympus. As you go down from the 11th floor, each level abuses the one below — pulling rank, belittling, using a dismissive tone.
>
> The situation has become worse since managed care has taken over. It was in this atmosphere that I became interested in the subject of humiliation in the workplace.
>
> I'm an assistant to a very dynamic doctor at the apex of the hierarchy. On more than one occasion, I've had to let her know

that even if she is stressed, she cannot talk to me in a demeaning way. It never ceases to amaze me how an individual can speak to one person with a tone of deep respect or deference, and then turn to another with completely different body language and a condescending tone. The affront to one's dignity is corrosive.

Once the CEO got upset about something he could not find, said something nasty to me on the phone and hung up. I called him back and told him that kind of behavior was out of the question if we were going to work together. I believe it is very important to establish guidelines to protect one's dignity.

Of course, the fact that I am not on a career track and will not be changing status makes it easier for me to do this. But I look forward to a time when bad treatment on the job will stand out for what it is, instead of simply being "the way it is."

"Human cooperation with mutual respect" is a simple idea that could transform the workplace. I can imagine a time when human resources departments would train all levels of employees, including top executives, with this as a goal. The irony is that they would get much better results if they adopted this approach.

After a decade at the firm, Grey suddenly finds himself beholden to an arbitrary, autocratic boss, brought in from outside. He writes:

My work style over the previous decade had been strongly collaborative, so nothing had prepared me for a domineering boss. The coping mechanisms I'd used in the past became worthless overnight. If I tried being passive in order to keep peace with him, he got worse. If I stood my ground, or if I raged back in anger — even justified anger — he got worse. When he was upset, he would glare at me so hideously, I could smell the sulfur of hell-fire.

About a year after he arrived, I began to feel that I was losing my mind. I blamed myself and became so desperate that I sought professional help. Without the aid of an excellent therapist, the support of loyal colleagues who were witness to my situation, and my church, I don't think I would have survived.

I also benefited from Internet resources, and books on coping with workplace bullying. In retrospect, I attribute my survival to my determination (1) not to be minimized, (2) to find the way back to my own dignity, and (3) to understand the dynamics of intimidating behavior and authoritarian organizations.

Gradually, I learned to respond to my abusive manager with poise and balance. The calmer and more centered I was, the more reckless he became. By keeping a detailed journal, I learned to anticipate his moves.

Finally, he precipitated a showdown, as a result of which his superiors saw him as I did, and fired him on the spot. I am still with the organization, and I fully love my work.

I am, however, profoundly changed. I see dysfunction around me, but no longer permit it to touch me. My life has new purpose because of what I overcame. In the aftermath of this crisis, I can now validate and help others who find themselves caught, as I was, in cycles of abuse and self-doubt.

Next, a story in which rank is pulled both on and by the teller of the tale. From a Foreign Service Officer turned novelist:

My father was a wealthy powerful executive, and a flagrant abuser of his rank, both at home as well as at work. A few examples:

- He loved to crack humiliating jokes.
- When, at the age of eight, I broke a drill bit while trying to do an assigned task, his response was, "Never send a boy to do a man's job."
- He dismissed my literary ambitions with the remark, "Art is merely for diversion," then complained, "Why can't you write like Morris West or Tom Clancy?"
- To my fifteen-year-old sister appearing before him in her first party dress, he commented, "Humph! Do you think you're a woman?"
- "Men who embrace are queers," was one of his typical pronouncements.

Naturally, I grew up with a loathing of arrogance. So it was quite a shock when I discovered that I myself am often guilty, at least in my heart, of pulling rank on others. In the last couple of decades, I've been reaching out more to different kinds of people, and in so doing have sometimes noticed I was secretly congratulating myself for practicing "the common touch!"

Another story involving self-awareness, from a graduate student in psychology:

Some time ago, I took my friend Susan out for dinner for her birthday. We ordered an appetizer and main courses, and soon both arrived at the same time. I was upset. Either the appetizer would go uneaten, or the salmon entrée would be cold by the time we got to it. I called the waitress over and began to express my displeasure. She suggested that she take the entrées back to the kitchen.

I could see what that would mean. The main dishes would sit back there and then she'd bring them out again in ten minutes, wilted and lukewarm. I looked her in the eye and told her I wouldn't accept such a solution. With my jaw set and using my most intimidating tone, I told her in no uncertain terms that if the entrées were not cooked fresh for us, I would be very unhappy. The implied threat couldn't have been clearer, and I felt so righteously justified about it.

While I was delivering my ultimatum, I glanced at my friend and saw she had a shocked look on her face. I suddenly realized, with stinging embarrassment, what I was doing. I was using my rank— as a customer to a "servant," and as an older woman to a much younger one — to put the waitress down, threatening her as if she were a child.

When she left the table I apologized to my friend, who said, "Don't apologize to me, apologize to her!" I couldn't bring myself to do it, and this has haunted me ever since. The episode made me much more aware of the workings of rank. I'm now less prone to pull rank when addressing people who are lower in rank than I am. The pain of remembering how people have put me down (I was a waitress myself when I was younger!), coupled with the shame that arises in me when I find myself doing the same thing, reminds me to have respect for the people I relate to.

Finally, this example from a retired police officer:

In the law enforcement and criminal justice communities, the rank structure is etched in stone. Ignoring it, even with the best intentions, can prove fatal on a personal and professional level, stripping one of dignity and livelihood.

As a young police detective, I chose to think outside the box and try to increase the professionalism and productivity of a department that was in desperate need of change. In doing so, I stepped on the toes of a number of high-ranking officials who were threatened by my recommendations, and it was made clear to me that I was a nobody and that RHIP (Rank Has Its Privileges). My seniors became so focused on undermining my actions and belittling me that I began to believe my ideas were flawed and without merit.

Upon consulting with legal counsel, I was informed that although the conduct being directed at me was wrong, it would be unwise to attempt to stop it or go public because doing so would show weakness of character. New policemen were expected to pay their dues as grunts in hopes of someday rising in the ranks.

After much suffering, the effects finally took their toll. In a community where I had once been recognized as a pillar of strength, I became a disgruntled cop stripped of dignity.

Years have passed now and I've regained my pride — not by attaining higher rank or proving that I am better than others, but by assisting those who have fallen victim to the same kind of abuse I did. It is my hope that by doing so and speaking out, I am contributing to the process of eliminating rankism from society. As with other social ills, this will take much time, dedication, and effort, but history has shown we can succeed. The nobodies of the world will prevail!

Chapter Nine

THE NOBODY REVOLUTION: OVERCOMING RANKISM

Nobodies' Liberation: A Joke or a Movement?

Until a group organizes and commands the power to compel equitable treatment, its members' rights can be, and usually are, ignored. It took the civil rights movement to combat racism. It took the women's movement to tackle sexism. Who is going to stand up for the nobodies?

Unlike blacks and women, nobodies are not an easily identifiable group. Not only do they share no visible trait, but they also have been nobodied in many quite different ways, some of them subtle and difficult to discern. And they nobody each other. But there's one important thing they all have in common: the experience of being dominated, degraded, exploited, or insulted by people with greater power than their own.

At first mention, the notion of Nobodies' Liberation sounds like a joke. It appears naive and utopian to imagine that nobodies might someday join together as a group and move the world to respect their dignity. The histories of the black and women's movements suggest, however, that what begins in the hearts of a few as an intimation of fairness and justice can become social reality within generations.

Nowadays, the fear of being labeled racist acts as a powerful deterrent to public and private acts of bigotry. Although accusations are sometimes unfounded, when they are true, the guilty lose promotions, jobs, rank. As groups of people who are being nobodied become adept at identifying and labeling the abuse they are suffering, an historic sea change will occur.

One new idea is needed to fuel this movement: that discrimination based on power disparities is no more justified than that based on differences in race or gender. One new word can ignite it: "rankism."

The process of discrediting rankism is likely to resemble the dismantling of the other isms. It will require both consciousness-raising and political action. Rankism will lose legitimacy as the cumulative result of many small changes in interpersonal relations and institutional practice. Most of these will probably occur within institutions and take the form of revisions to by-laws and practices that determine the sharing of power.

It is never possible to pinpoint in advance the particular group that will initiate a revolution. Given that caveat, it is possible to spot a few potential candidates. Following are two that might kindle a revolt of nobodies — one in the field of education, the other in organized religion.

Graduate teaching assistants today bear a disproportionate share of the teaching burden of well-compensated tenured faculty, yet they are hardly paid a living wage. Many accept this, as their predecessors have for generations, because they still believe there is a good prospect of someday getting tenure themselves. But today, in truth, there is not. With the repeal of mandatory retirement age at 65, senior professors are staying on into their seventies. Tenured positions are becoming scarce. It is not uncommon for hundreds of fully qualified Ph.D.s to apply for a single tenure track position. This is a volatile situation, ripe for revolution. But it remains to be seen whether graduate teaching assistants will organize on behalf of narrow professional goals and settle for a sliver of the pie, or whether they will be a voice for more inclusive, more participatory governance in education in general.

A second hotspot is the incipient rebellion among the Roman Catholic laity, galvanized by the scandal of sexual abuse by their clergy. A group called the "Voice of the Faithful" is seeking to establish a measure of democracy in a church that has long insisted on the pre-eminence of an authoritarian hierarchy. Using the Internet as an organizing tool, it has attracted a rapidly growing membership from all over the United States, and many other countries as well.

Nobodies' Liberation has yet to find its Elizabeth Cady Stanton and Susan B. Anthony, its Rosa Parks, or its Martin Luther King, Jr. — though if ever there were a movement that should eschew hero worship, it's this one. But even without such leaders, more and more nobodies are beginning to stand up for themselves and their fellow citizens. They are risking their station to preserve their integrity.

In the aftermath of the September 11th terrorist attacks and corporate accounting scandals, many whistleblowers who might have once been dismissed as uppity nobodies have instead been acclaimed as heroes. These examples notwithstanding, the National Whistleblower Center in Washington reports that most employees who expose rankist practices in the workplace still face on-the-job harassment or unfair discipline, and it recommends legislation to protect them.

Nobodies, unlike the other Invisibles, have not embraced identity politics for themselves because they are inclined to acquiesce in society's view that they have no identity. But think for a moment what would happen if, instead of pulling rank on each other, they took aim at rankism itself. The concluding scene in the film "Revenge of the Nerds" is a fanciful depiction of what might ensue if "nerds" did not remain passive when one of their number was singled out for bullying, but rather joined forces in his or her defense.

In the past, we have thought of an "equalizer" as a weapon. In the future, the most effective "equalizing weapon" may be the Internet, with its potential for mobilizing allies who share a common predicament. Nobodies can only succeed if they coordinate their efforts to overcome oppression. The children's book *Yertle the Turtle* by Dr. Seuss graphically demonstrates the extreme dependence of power-holders on the nobodies who support them.

So imagine a few nobodies, unaffiliated with any existing identity group, joining the Parade of Invisibles, falling in behind a phalanx of people with disabilities. At first, there is only a trickle of them. Now imagine that a group of somebodies, realizing they themselves are once and future nobodies, join the march as well. The contingent of nobodies slowly swells; the trickle becomes a stream. And when kids and students add their presence, the stream becomes a river. Eventually, there are more marchers than spectators. The somebodies watching from the sidelines begin to feel left out. Now they, too, feel like nobodies, and merge with the parade. In the end, no one stands aloof or pulls rank; no one shrinks back or grovels.

Perhaps a band strikes up a tune, and with the "Anthem of the Nobodies" reverberating through the streets, African-Americans, Hispanic-Americans, Asian-Americans, feminists, seniors, gays, and others all march in stride — not as members of disparate identity groups, but as individual human beings, now fully visible for the very first time.

Here is a telling story from a woman who works as a consultant to small businesses:

> As a child, I used to play a game with my little brother. I would tell him I could cast a spell on him to make him invisible. Then I pretended I couldn't see him, and he really believed me! I told him he would be able to see himself in the mirror, and that the cleaning lady would be able to see him. Despite those exceptions, he still thought the spell was working, and would get terribly upset. I was delighted with myself and my power over him. I told my girlfriend, and then we played the game on her little brother, too.

With the appearance of the nobodies, the last of the Invisibles are out of the closet, insisting upon their personal dignity regardless of current rank, power, or status. In calling his saga *Les Misérables*, Victor Hugo was referring to the entire French people. The last of the Invisibles — the nobodies — constitute the whole human race.

The Nobody Manifesto

Who are the nobodies? Those with less power. At the moment.

Who are the somebodies? Those with more power. At the moment. Power is signified by rank. Rank in a particular setting. Somebodies hold higher rank than nobodies. In that setting. For that moment.

A somebody in one setting can be a nobody in another, and vice versa. A somebody now might be a nobody a moment later, and vice versa.

Abuse of the power inherent in rank is rankism. When somebodies use the power of their position in one setting to exercise power in another, that's rankism. When somebodies use the power of their position to put a permanent hold on their power, that, too, is rankism.

Dignity is innate, nonnegotiable, and inviolate. No person's dignity is any less worthy of respect, any less sacred than anyone else's. Equal dignity requires equal opportunity. Rankism is an indefensible abridgment of the dignity of nobodies, and a stain on the honor of somebodies.

As once and future nobodies, we're all potential victims of rankism. As would-be somebodies, we're all potential perpetrators. Securing equal dignity means overcoming rankism.

Who are the nobodies? They are Everyman, Everywoman, Everychild. Each of us in our secret dreams of becoming someone new, something more. The nobodies are us. Therein lies our power.

Nobodies of the world, unite! We have nothing to lose but our shame.

The Invisibles Become Visible

The idea of nobodies joining the Parade of Invisibles en masse is probably as fanciful as the notion of the march itself. As a metaphor, however, the parade is instructive. Its successive groups of participants have found pride in the very traits used by others to handicap them in the struggle for recognition, and they have gone on to build effective movements defined by those traits. When it comes to building a movement, however, it's obvious that nobodies have some inherent handicaps.

Again, they share no observable characteristics, such as black skin, female gender, or a physical disability. Furthermore, their lack of solidarity means they can be picked off one at a time. Nobodies are outsiders — the opposite of joiners. Without joiners, how can there be a movement?

But nobodies have one thing going for them: anyone can become a nobody, and sooner or later almost everyone does. There is no one who, with a bit of consideration and foresight, cannot imagine being in the club.

Many people are born into Nobodyland and never find a way out. Others are nobodied during their schooling. The end of a relationship, a divorce, an illness, or bereavement can send people there, often without warning. Downsizing has made nobodies of countless individuals, and economic globalization heralds periods of nobodyness for many more in the years to come.

In addition, some people find themselves in Nobodyland for a spell, as I did, while recovering from burnout. A stint as a nobody at one time or another during our lives is becoming ever more likely, either by chance or by choice. Regardless of how one gets there, Nobodyland can be a desolate place.

The reality is that we are all enmeshed simultaneously in dozens of distinct but overlapping pecking orders. It is not only others who view us in such terms; we see *ourselves* this way as well. An interior version of the struggle for recognition mirrors the exterior one.

Remember the retired pharmaceutical executive who felt like a nobody without his job and title? Well, his story has a surprise ending.

I decided to create a fictitious organization — The Mission and Values Institute — thinking it might give me "card credibility." This led to an interesting experiment in which I used either my "nobody card," or a card with a title and my sham affiliation.

The results? Very different responses! Over time, two things emerged.

First, I became much more comfortable with myself without a title and organization. And great self-worth had a big impact on how others perceived me.

Second, I discovered a very important subset of people who did not use title and organization as their initial introduction, and found they were more interesting to me than the rest.

The lesson is that the cards we carry can open many doors, and those with the loftiest titles and most prestigious organizations give the bearer the most instant access. However, instant access to many doors does not have as much long-term value as the development of lasting relationships with people whom you really respect and enjoy.

Even the grandest somebodies have nobodies within. We all know people considered by others to be nobodies, who nonetheless comport themselves like kings and queens. Both the nobody and the somebody have vital roles to play in our inner lives, just as these aspects of our personas do in the public arena. Neither our private nor our public self can do its part without the other. The attempt to eradicate the nobody within and consistently present ourselves as somebody has unhappy consequences for both ourselves and others.

To overcome our ingrained antipathy to Nobodyland, we must learn to see its gateway as a revolving door, through which we can come and go. As the hobgoblins of Nobodyland lose their grip on us, the contours of a world with equal dignity for all come into focus. When we accept the nobody within us, we lose the impulse to nobody others. When we identify the somebody inside, we tap into our capacity to make a public contribution.

Nobodies' Liberation probably won't look like the movements that have preceded it. Don't expect any "million-nobody marches." But in one respect, Nobodies' Lib is likely to mirror the identity-based movements. The idea of Nobodies' Liberation will slowly and irreversibly remold our psyches, undercutting the somebody mystique until it has lost its hold on us. We are in the midst of a profound shift that will end by making the infringement of each other's dignity unthinkable.

Humor, Etiquette, and Golden Rules

Do unto others as you would have them do unto you.
 – The Golden Rule

What you do not want done to yourself, do not do to others.
 – Confucius

What you do unto the least of them, you do unto me.
 — Jesus

We should behave to our friends, as we would wish our friends to behave to us.
 ——Aristotle

Act only on that maxim through which you can at the same time will that it should become a universal law.
 — Immanuel Kant's Categorical Imperative

The indignities we inflict on others and those inflicted on us build until they erupt in indignation. The remedy for this is as simple as it is ancient: protect the dignity of others as you would your own.

I never expected the golden rule to make an appearance in this analysis, but there it is. Philosophers and prophets have been advocating it, in one form or another, for millennia. The golden rule has many variants, and the people who formulated them, far from being utopian dreamers, were all expressing a profound insight: that rank abuse contains the seeds of its own curtailment. In spite of the pessimism and cynicism of their times, they realized that inequity generates an unending series of retaliatory countermeasures which, in turn, create pressure to make contests for rank and recognition more fair. They foresaw that equilibrium would be reached only when everyone enjoyed equal protection against indignity and injustice.

In a world in which rankism has lost its sanction, nobodies and somebodies will be accorded equal respect as people, notwithstanding the fact that aptitudes, skills, and talents continue to show wide individual variations. Furthermore, somebodies and nobodies will be regularly exchanging places. We might continue to call those at the top of a particular ladder of rank somebodies and those at the bottom nobodies. But we will do so without the old expectation that somebodies are at liberty to parlay their current success into a permanent hold on power. The portentous VIP overtones of the somebody label will eventually disappear. When we come to anticipate that nobodies in one realm or at one time will be somebodies under different circumstances, nobodies will lose their dunce caps, somebodies their top hats and tiaras, and the somebody mystique will fade into oblivion.

Under these circumstances, the terms "somebody" and "nobody" will lose their charge, and come to refer simply to public and private, respectively. We will think of somebodies more as draftees, temporarily serving tours of duty in open view as leaders, exemplars, public figures. If we find ourselves serving as a somebody we won't fall for our new "uniform," nor will others. There will be no pulling rank when we have it and no servility when we don't, because rank will be understood to signify expertise in some well-defined, limited area, not as an opportunity or excuse for self-aggrandizement. Somebodies and nobodies will be seen as organic complements, co-existing within society as well as within each one of us.

Deep down, everyone knows that somebodies pay for their fame in lost autonomy, but we're eager to sign up nonetheless as insurance against being nobodied. The desire for fame is, in actuality, largely defensive; the price is to efface one's individuality and serve the group as a role model and exemplar.

In contrast, nobodies can simply be themselves. Off-stage, out of the spotlight, they are free to experiment, to fail, and to change. It's a paradox, but while nobodies dream of being somebodies, somebodies dream of the opposite, because it is in our capacity as nobodies that we create and feel most alive.

In a world where rankism is the exception rather than the rule, targets of intentional abuse will become rare. We will keep our word to those of lower rank, just as we do to those of higher rank. Some people may still feel like nobodies, but no shame will attach to that, and barriers impeding changes of rank will be dissolved.

Rules that are not enforced usually go unheeded. The golden rule is no exception. Although it encapsulates the corrective to rankism in powerful, evocative language, it is often ignored by secular and religious people alike. Had we honored the golden rule there would have been no need for the civil rights movement.

Both spirituality and politics have a role to play in changing human behavior. Spiritual principles such as the golden rule point to an ideal and serve as a simple test for when we are falling short of it; political ones, supported by pressure from the populace and legislation, hold us accountable. They enforce the golden rule. The history of the struggles against racism and sexism suggest that as nobodies identify abuses of rank, refuse to put up with insults and disdain, and exorcise servility from their behavior, those who would demean them will become more circumspect and gradually find themselves coming into compliance with the golden rule.

Humor is sure to help catalyze this change. It's no accident that rank, like race and gender, lies at the heart of many jokes and cartoons. A boss sitting behind his big desk is about to fire a subordinate, when *his* boss ominously summons him over the intercom. A bum hawks T-shirts with his own image on them. A group of craven-looking cavemen urges one of their number to inform their leader — busy sharpening his spear — that he is guilty of crimes against humanity. One king confides to another that theology holds no interest for him apart from the doctrine of the divine right of kings.

Humor has always been a way of exploring and defusing the stigmas that attach to different pieces of our personal identities. Rank-based humor, like its race and gender-based cousins, runs the gamut from good-natured to caustic and cruel. Social and political satirists perform a civic function in this regard: by exposing abuse to the light, they help keep it in check. Comedians who joke about the excesses of rank deflate the tendency to self-aggrandizement. When humor about nobodies and somebodies proliferates and cuts closer to the bone, we'll know that rankism is losing its legitimacy. We joke about the rhino in the room as a prelude to open discussion; but when we can stand back and laugh at old dichotomies, they will have lost their power to divide.

Etiquette has always been a repository of the social consensus on rank. Traditional manners protect historical prerogatives and shore up the somebody mystique. Just as the advent of egalitarian race and gender consciousness had an impact on etiquette, so too will the development of an egalitarian consciousness with regard to rank. Not long ago, servers in restaurants were summoned with a shout of "Waiter!" or "Boy!" or, in France, "Garçon!" Now, the norm has become the more respectful "Sir?" Etiquette helps prevent interpersonal insults, but it is not up to the task of leading the way to a new consensus on universal dignity. Once that is achieved, however, etiquette can help to consolidate it.

As was the case with racism and sexism, there will inevitably be an awkward transition period during which new manners are shaped by conscious application of principles of political correctness. As first, somebodies can be expected to bend over backwards to avoid the slightest hint of misusing their rank. Gradually, a new, less self-conscious but more egalitarian code of manners will evolve based on reciprocal, respectful appreciation, independent of whether people's current roles are prominent or behind-the-scenes, executive or supportive, public or private. The trend toward informality evidenced in Internet communications may be one sign of diminishing deference to old hierarchies. A *New Yorker* cartoon shows a pooch at a computer saying, "On the Internet, nobody knows you're a dog."

An Internet entrepreneur who changed her name in her forties writes:

> My name change from the diminutive "Patty" to "Ryan" seems a transition to the more adult "me," and it works to my benefit, especially on the Internet. Many people have adopted gender-neutral names on-line. One may look for clues to the person's gender but ultimately it is freeing not to know, because in real life so much of rank gets played out based on gender, height, stature, looks, disabilities, etc.
>
> With "Ryan," most people on the net assume I am male, and I think that works to my advantage.

In a world in which rankism is stripped of its sanction, nobodies and somebodies will look upon each other without envy or disdain, aware that public recognition, or the lack of it, simply reflects different social roles. The nobody and somebody within will become friends and partners. The cult of celebrity (Michael Jordan, Madonna, Michael Jackson, and Princess Diana) will look as silly as the cult of personality (Stalin, Mao, Ceauçescu, and Mobutu).

Political Realignment

From ancient to modern times, nothing has shaped people's political orientation more than their relationship to rank. Accordingly, significant reorderings of rank have invariably resulted in political realignment. For example, the collapse of the American segregationist consensus, in which whites were deemed to outrank blacks, brought political realignment to many regions of the country.

So, too, we can anticipate a similar effect following the dissolution of the somebody mystique. The explanation for this lies in the psychological inclinations that determine how people affiliate themselves politically.

Labels like liberal and conservative, left and right, Democrat and Republican change their meanings over time. Here I use the words liberal and conservative as they are commonly understood now at the turn of the twentieth century in the United States. In this context, liberals tend to be more suspicious of authority and rank, conservatives more accepting and supportive. Conservatives see authority inherent in rank as commanding obedience, whereas the instincts of liberals are to "question authority."

In psychological terms, liberals tend to identify more with the nobody within — hence their sympathy for the underdog. Their aversion to the abuse of rank can prevent them from appreciating its legitimate uses. Conservatives, on the other hand, identify more with the somebody within and therefore tend to align themselves politically with those of higher status. Their insistence on the prerogatives of rank can blind them to instances of its misuse. If they are to work together constructively, liberals must learn to recognize the value of rank as an indicator of excellence, and conservatives must be more principled about limiting the reach of rank to its proper sphere. Doing this is not easy, but it's the essence of nonpartisanship.

The right is the party that defends rank. The left is the party that defends the weak against rankism. Is it any wonder that politics weaves back and forth in an endless zigzag between these two complementary policy poles? A society that does not accord rank its due loses its ability to coordinate complex tasks in a timely fashion; it may even fall into the tyranny of structurelessness (anarchy). A society that does not subject rank to vigilant scrutiny will find its liberty eroded and its evolution slowed; it may even revert to the tyranny of conformity (autocracy). The teeter-totter between right and left — between closing ranks and breaking ranks — is endemic to politics everywhere, and reflects the need to avoid these two extremes, either of which can prove fatal. Sartorial fashions mirror this same pattern, shifting from formal to casual and then back again in an eternal ebb and flow.

As rank is shorn of rankism, the distance between right and left will narrow, and liberal and conservative positions on matters now in dispute will become more alike. New issues that involve the proper use of authority and rank will arise and split the electorate into right and left, but along new fissures. An eternal political seesaw will reflect this continual process, with perpetual alternations between the unfettered use of new powers and their circumscription through institutionalization of accountability.

In a world of inviolate dignity, unblinkered by the somebody mystique, nobodies will not so easily be persuaded to vote against their own economic interests in the name of upholding authority and preserving order. How, then, will equal dignity translate into political policy? The non-negotiable demands of a dignitarian movement are likely to include a living wage, universal health care, and quality education for all. Until everyone has these basic necessities, some will be competing for rank and recognition with serious handicaps, and the egalitarian promise imprinted on the American psyche by Thomas Jefferson will go unfulfilled.

Education is also crucial to the liberation of the protesters marching in the streets of third world cities. Their lives of chronic indignity make them easy targets for demagogues fanning fears of modernity. The impact of education ranges from undercutting such demagogic manipulation to reducing fertility and child mortality rates to protection against HIV-AIDS. As Jefferson knew, a well-educated citizenry is a prerequisite to effective democracy.

Liberté, *Dignité*, Égalité, Fraternité

Democratic nations have been faulted for pursuing liberty at the expense of equality. As democracy displaces the autocracies that still govern many social institutions within these nations, attention is bound to fall on the gap between the rich and the poor. This economic gap — within nations and between them as well — poses a threat to good conscience. When the disparity can be traced to rankism, then the associated gap in dignity is inflammatory.

Communist doctrine focused on class conflict and dictated the equitable redistribution of wealth. In the name of economic justice, communism built a variety of regimes, all of them undemocratic and rankist in the extreme. Communist governments everywhere met with intense internal resistance. The dream of economic justice went unrealized and, more often than not, turned into the nightmare of life in a police state. The failure of these regimes strongly suggests there are no routes to economic justice that do not respect human dignity.

A rank-based strategy aimed at equalizing dignity stands in sharp contrast to the class-based Marxist strategy aimed at equalizing wealth. In practice, communism merely created a new elite, which arrogated wealth to itself. A rank-based strategy anticipates rather the redistribution of recognition and respect in the wake of a dispelled somebody mystique.

This book does not present or advance a particular philosophy of justice. Rather, it focuses on rank and its abuses as a strategy for overcoming injustice. This strategy, adapted from identity politics, is compatible with a variety of philosophical visions, including, for example, those of John Rawls (*A Theory of Justice*), Michael Walzer (*Spheres of Justice*), and Avishai Margalit (*The Decent Society*). The emphasis is on incremental democratic means, not grand moral ends.

Rather than ask what justice would look like, it asks why people accede to injustice, why they acquiesce in indignity. It sees dignity as a halfway house to justice, and identifies the principal impediment to equal dignity as rankism. Put another way, it sees a world of equal dignity as a steppingstone to the more just, fair, and decent societies that political philosophers and theorists like those above have envisioned and delineated. Taking a page from the identity-based movements, it suggests that the way to build a just society is to organize a dignitarian movement against rankism.

Americans are apt to proselytize democracy in its American form — a two-party system, periodic elections, checks and balances, independent judiciary — unaware that this is but one of many possible mechanisms to protect against authoritarianism. The real goal, the human goal, is not to install this or any other version of democracy, but rather to curtail rankism. American democracy is but one means to that goal. No particular implementation of democracy is an end in itself. Different societies will adopt different means for ensuring the efficacy of rank while protecting against the abuses of rankism.

The fundamental human truth with which non-rankist governance structures must conform is that *dignity is not negotiable*. Rank and dignity are independent in principle, and must be disconnected in practice.

As a dignitarian movement gathers momentum, the right to dignity will take its place in the pantheon of human rights. The passion for equality that de Tocqueville observed in American democracy will get equal billing with the love of liberty. Just because America has yet to deliver on Jefferson's promise, does not mean it can't or won't.

On the eve of World War II, the British novelist E. M. Forster wrote a famous essay entitled *Two Cheers for Democracy* — "One because it admits variety and two because it permits criticism." Even though western democracy was under assault by fascism, Forster concluded that "Two cheers are quite enough: there is no occasion to give three."

Forster reserved his third cheer for a mythical state of felicity that he referred to as "Love, the Beloved Republic." That does indeed seem out of reach. But, if the bridge of Dignity sees us from Liberty to Justice, can Fraternity lie far beyond? When dignity is secure, near and far, here and now, French revolutionary ideals begin to sound considerably less utopian. On that occasion, surely Mr. Forster would not begrudge democracy his third hurrah.

The notion of rankism is the bridge that links two revolutions of the twentieth century — civil rights and human rights. The civil rights movement offers the methods and energy of identity politics to the moral campaign for human rights. Combined to form a dignitarian movement against rankism, the political movement for civil rights and the moral campaign for human rights complete and fortify each other. A dignitarian movement provides a nonviolent, democratic approach to the daunting and inescapable challenge of the twenty-first century — global economic justice.

POSTSCRIPT

The following four articles were written after the first publication of *Somebodies and Nobodies* and indicate how the ideas in the book can be applied to a variety of social and political problems. Since they were written for different purposes and to stand alone, there is some overlap.

What Really Divides Us*

The Supreme Court decision upholding the University of Michigan Law School's use of race in admission has stirred up an all-too-familiar controversy. By what means can we deliver on Thomas Jefferson's proposition that "all men are created equal?"

Without question, affirmative action has given teeth to the goal of equal opportunity. But it alone cannot bring about the society envisaged by Jefferson because it fails to address a problem more fundamental than racism, sexism, and the variety of other "isms" that still plague us. What underlies *all* these forms of discrimination is something less conspicuous than race or gender, but no less profound in its consequences. It is rank — in particular, low rank signifying a lack of power.

The primary rift dividing the citizens of democracies today — one that cries out for attention — is not that of race, gender, age, or religion. Rather, it is the gap between the "somebodies" — the relatively powerful and successful — and the "nobodies" — the relatively weak and vulnerable. The nobodies are not just another in the litany of identity groups. There's something different about this one because each and

*This article appeared in *Newsday*, August 3, 2003.

every one of us has been a member, just as all of us have nominated others for inclusion.

It happens everywhere, every day. A boss harasses an employee; a customer demeans a waiter; a doctor disparages a nurse; a teacher humiliates a student; students ostracize other students; a parent belittles a child. Somebodies with higher rank and more power in any given setting can maintain an environment that is hostile and demeaning to nobodies with lower rank and less power in that setting, much as most everywhere whites used to be at liberty to mistreat blacks.

Some 35 years of affirmative action have put racists and sexists on notice. But there has been no corresponding outcry against abuses that occur *within* a race or gender. Blacks insult and exploit other blacks of lower rank, whites do the same to whites, and women to women, all with confidence that it will pass as business as usual.

We don't have a name for abuse and discrimination based on rank, but we need one. When discrimination and injustice are race-based, we call it racism; when they're gender-based, we call it sexism. By analogy, rank-based abuse and exploitation can be called "rankism." Naming rankism, putting it in the spotlight, can be half the battle.

Rankism occurs when rank-holders use the power of their position to secure unwarranted advantages or benefits for themselves. It typically takes the form of self-aggrandizement and exploitation of subordinates, that is, of rule violations by those in positions of power to serve their own ends. It is the opposite of service. Good leaders eschew rankism; bad ones indulge in it. It can be found in government, businesses, families, workplaces, schools and universities, as well as religious, nonprofit, and healthcare organizations. It distorts personal relationships, erodes the will to learn, fosters disease, taxes productivity, undermines public trust, stokes ethnic hatred, and incites revenge. Recent front-page examples include corporate and philanthropic corruption, sexual abuse by clergy, school hazing and abuse of elders.

At the societal level, rank-based discrimination afflicts none more inescapably than those lacking the protections of social rank — the working poor. Two recent books chronicle this widening fissure. In *Nickel and Dimed: On (Not) Getting By in America*, Barbara Ehrenreich makes a compelling case that the working poor are in effect unacknowledged benefactors whose labor subsidizes those who are more advantaged. In *Wealth and Democracy: A Political History of the American Rich*, Kevin Phillips explores how the rich and politically powerful create and perpetuate privilege at the expense of the middle and lower classes.

I am in no way proposing that we do away with rank. That would make about as much sense as trying to do away with race or gender in order to fight racism or sexism. When earned and exercised appropriately, rank is a legitimate, virtually indispensable tool of organization. But when the high-ranking abuse their authority, those of lower rank experience discrimination and injustice not different in their material and psychological effects from the discrimination and injustice we now disallow when their victims belong to the familiar identity groups.

To achieve a just society, we have to decide what it means to be a nation of equals. Indeed, at first glance, such a goal might seem absurd. How can we be equals when we are obviously unequal in skill, talent, beauty, strength, health, wealth or any other commonly recognized trait? The answer is that people are equal in a sense they have always considered fundamental to being human. They are equal in dignity.

This is not some utopian ideal. As Vartan Gregorian, president of the Carnegie foundation in New York, puts it, "Dignity is not negotiable." Rankism is invariably an insult to the dignity of an individual or group. If the aggrieved party dare not protest, it will nurse its wounds until a time when it can exact revenge. The twentieth century has seen numerous demagogues who have promised to restore the pride and dignity of a people who felt they'd been "nobodied." The long-term and most horrific consequences of rankism between peoples range from sabotage and terrorism to genocide and war.

One may wonder whether rankism is part of human nature. Not so long ago, it was widely believed that racism and sexism were, but now they are generally regarded as learned. While the impulse to exploit a power advantage for personal gain is hardly uncommon in our species, history shows it is equally in our nature to detest such abuses and to act together to circumscribe the authority of rank-holders.

To this end, we have overthrown kings and tyrants and placed political power in the hands of the people. We have reined in monopolies with antitrust legislation. We have limited the power of employers through unionization. Blacks, women, homosexuals and people with disabilities have all built effective movements that succeeded in replacing a once-sacrosanct social consensus with another that repudiated it.

People acquiesce to rankism because they fear the consequences of resisting: demerit, demotion, ridicule and ostracism. The muffled complaints, occasional whistle-blowing and sporadic outbursts we do hear echo those of blacks and women who resisted in solitary protest before popular movements made it impossible to ignore their demands.

The identity-group movements created the safety in numbers that persuaded millions of oppressed individuals to stop putting up with discrimination. As the costs of rankism are exposed and it loses social sanction, its victims will likewise join forces and make themselves heard. A striking example is the lay Catholic organization Voice of the Faithful, whose goal is to limit the absolute authority of clerics. In time we may see the emergence of a broad-based "dignitarian" movement dedicated to overcoming rankism in all its guises.

Today's n-word is "nobody." The successes of affirmative action have brought us to a time in which victims of indignity, injustice, and inequity are as apt to be white as black, male as female, or straight as gay. What primarily marks people for mistreatment and exploitation now is low rank and the powerlessness it signifies. Overcoming rankism is democracy's next step. In taking it, we will have the opportunity to honor the dual commitment to both freedom *and* justice that our nation's founders imprinted on the American psyche.

Rankism in the Workplace:
The Hidden Barrier to Success*

Organizations, like organisms, are vulnerable to maladies. They are especially prone to develop those endemic to society as a whole. For example, so long as racism and sexism were undiagnosed and untreated at large, they found many businesses to be hospitable hosts. In the aftermath of the civil rights and women's movements, most firms became alert to the symptoms of these afflictions. A company caught harboring either of them today faces the choice of remedying the situation or losing business.

There's another malady to which hierarchical organizations are susceptible, but which has yet to be identified and named. It is the abuse of power by those higher up on the totem pole in relation to those lower down. When discrimination and injustice are race-based, we call it racism; when they're gender-based, we call it sexism. By analogy, "rankism" is defined as abuse or discrimination based on the differences of power attached to rank.

New words are often slow to win their way into the lexicon, but once they do, the ramifications can be great. The coinage "sexism" was at first vehemently resisted, especially by those who were practicing it. Isolating and naming a problem can be a big part of finding a solution to it.

Once we have done so with rankism, we see examples of it everywhere. Officers abuse suspects. Team coaches bully players. School principals insult teachers. Professors exploit teaching assistants. Caretakers mistreat invalids. Cooks demean servers. All are forms of this insidious scourge.

Since hierarchies are all about rank and power, it's not surprising that they are the primary incubators of rankism. The power vested in rank-holders at each level of a hierarchy gives them leverage over those of lower rank, shielding them from the consequences of exploiting subordinates or shareholders for personal advantage. Sooner or later

*This is an abridged version of an article that appeared in Canada's national newspaper, the *Globe and Mail*, November 23, 2003.

those with high rank are tempted to use their position for self-aggrandizement and personal gain instead of the institution's avowed purpose. A recent example was the board-approved $180 million compensation package awarded to the Chairman of the New York Stock Exchange.

Like racism and sexism, rankism can cripple an organization, sometimes fatally. Nonprofits are equally vulnerable. Typically they start out with the intention of doing good and providing a service. But like a parasitical disease, rankism can subvert that purpose to the quite different goal of advancing the personal security of those at the top. The organization's focus gradually shifts from public service to self-preservation and the personal interests of its leadership.

The effects of rankism on its victims are similar to those of racism or sexism on minorities and women. Abuse and discrimination feel disrespectful, demeaning, and degrading to victims no matter what the excuse — race, religion, gender, age, sexual orientation or rank. In contrast to the other now-familiar "isms," it plays no favorites, striking across the board from day workers to the highest echelons of management.

Early detection and prompt treatment of rankism can restore worker morale, rejuvenate disillusioned executives, and improve a company's bottom line. Maintaining a strong organizational defense against rankism is practically synonymous with good management. In *Good to Great: Why Some Companies Make the Leap … and Others Don't*, Jim Collins makes the point that protecting their firms from abuses of rank and the indignity such practices sow is the hallmark of great business leaders.

Under duress, people may seem to compromise their dignity, but they are only temporizing, awaiting the first opportunity to demand the respect that everyone wants and deserves. Once the rank and file begin withholding their hearts and minds — as they do from any organization beset with rankism — the enterprise begins to decline.

None other than George Washington had this insight with respect to slavery, one of the most noxious forms of rankism. Today the inefficiency of slavery is obvious. But to Washington, himself a slave-owner, it came as a surprise. While on a visit to Philadelphia, he noticed that free men there could do in "two or three days what would employ [his slaves] a month or more." His explanation that slaves had no chance "to establish a good name [and so were] too regardless of a bad one" was not that of a moralizer, but rather of a practical man concerned with the bottom line.

Rankism won't yield to preaching, but it will diminish as it becomes clear that rankist practices undermine creativity, productivity, customer service and employee commitment. Learning not to demean workers is as beneficial to the success of a business as is realizing that "the customer is king."

Today employers are not dealing with slaves, though it is sometimes argued that wage-earners are wage-slaves and salaried employees only marginally more independent. But the negative motivation of the past — fear of penalties or job loss — is now becoming dwarfed by the positive incentive of being part of a team of responsible professionals. Eliminating "recognition deficiencies" in the workplace will be as good for the bottom line as eliminating nutritional deficiencies was for the productivity of day laborers.

As rankism is identified and reduced, people's energy becomes catalyzed and engaged. Employees who feel recognized as individuals and who feel they have a fair chance at promotion give their companies their best. Organizations that figure out how to give their workers a voice in management and a stake in its profitability reap great benefits.

The competitive advantages of relatively non-rankist hierarchies are most easily discernible in institutions devoted to research and development, where the very purpose of the enterprise is to discover and exploit new ideas. Such organizations are more likely to recognize the stifling effects of rankism and build a culture in which preventing it is paramount. For example, Intel, like many technology firms, operates with the explicit understanding that any employee is free to call into question any other employee's professional views. A newly-hired twenty-year-old can challenge a director of research or the CEO. The policy of open, free exchange regardless of rank is seen as a vital part of keeping the company a creative, productive place. Rankism is perceived as a threat to research. Condescension and arrogance are out. Open, reciprocal interaction is valued over pride of position.

In a tragic irony, those who stoically put up with a rankist environment often do so because they covet for themselves the rewards that come with status and power and dream of someday attaining them. But so long as rankism persists, the chances of this happening are slim. In truth such individuals are supporting the very system that is keeping them down. It is only when rankism is dismantled that they have a genuine shot at advancing instead of just illusions of doing so.

The problem is not with authority per se, but with its abuse. Making the distinction between rank and rankism actually revalidates rank when it has been properly earned. Sorting out the proper and improper uses of rank restores to it the respect it deserves. In the absence of rankism, presidents, CEOs, and leaders of every kind gain the recognition that is their due — no more, no less. The only real "boss" is a better idea or a better question.

The generation now entering the workforce is notably less willing to put up with unfair treatment than any of its predecessors. Today's young are mobile, resourceful, multi-skilled and more ready than were their parents to take chances. They are groping toward a new set of principles by which recognition is sought — principles that downplay rigid hierarchy and status and affirm the notions of equal dignity, teamwork and a more equitable distribution of rewards.

These attitudes herald a major transformation of the workplace. Just as in the civic realm subjects evolved into citizens, likewise in the realm of work we can anticipate employees evolving into partners.

In a post-rankist workplace, rank will be awarded and held in relation to a particular task. Recognition will be given upon the completion of that task, and rank then reassigned as needed to facilitate cooperation on another project. Although it's long been a fixture of compensation packages, the correlation between responsibility for decision making and salary will be reexamined. Asking a good question — one that spares the firm the consequences of a bad decision — is as important to the bottom line as is making a good decision.

To retain the loyalty of their co-workers, executives will take care to neither show favoritism to those of high rank nor abridge the privileges of those lower down. Companies will take pride in being places where everyone experiences equal dignity, has equal opportunity, and receives equal justice. The mailroom-to-boardroom story will become less exceptional; employee co-owners, with a share of the equity, will become more common; and the income and equity gaps between the highest and lowest paid will narrow.

Firms of the future will incorporate into their business plans scenarios for their employees' advancement. In a post-rankist environment, personnel will be seen less as workers holding down a job and more as learners progressing to different levels. In order to create room at the top so others have a chance for upward mobility, resources will be devoted to "graduating" executives. Personnel officers will assume responsibility for seeing that everyone in the firm has somewhere to go, whether inside or outside the company, and assist them in these transitions.

Although rankism can't be eradicated overnight, it can be put on notice as we've done with other kinds of prejudice and discrimination. Authority can be democratized while simultaneously increasing organizational efficiency not only in our civic institutions but in the workplace as well. The nations that curtailed rankism in government led the world in the 20th century. The nations that are most successful in removing rankism from the workplace will lead in the 21st.

Recognition and Martyrdom

What do school dropouts, computer hackers and suicide bombers have in common? They all suffer from "recognition disorders."

Recognition is the meat and potatoes of our identity. It is as indispensable to mental health as food is to physical health.

A baby's cry commands recognition from the day it's born. Toddlers demand it from adults, making their parents' lives miserable until they get it. Adolescents show off, even take insane risks, to extract it from their peers. Adults risk their reputations and sacrifice their health in its pursuit.

Like nutritional deficiencies, recognition deficiencies can stunt growth and impair performance. As their hunger for recognition mounts, those who feel invisible become increasingly desperate. What begins as a deficiency congeals into full-blown pathology. Like their nutritional counterpart — eating disorders — recognition disorders can prove fatal.

The English writer John Fowles warns, "The sense that you are nobody can drive you to violence and unreason. Through all human history it has been the hidden motive — that unbearable desire to prove oneself somebody — behind countless insanities and acts of violence." A confidant of one of the Columbine students who killed a dozen of their schoolmates in 2000 said of his friend, "He was afraid he would never be known." His sentiment brings to mind William James's observation that "The deepest principle of human nature is the craving to be appreciated."

Acknowledgment from others gives shape and coherence to our identities. It is through the give and take of recognition that we define ourselves as individuals, build integrity and develop a sense of dignity. Recognition confirms identity and affirms dignity. Contrariwise, removal of the integrative effects of recognition, as happens in the extreme with solitary confinement, causes our identity to become unglued and is experienced as a loss of dignity. Deprivation of dignity breeds indignation, and with indignation, a martyr is born.

Today the word "martyr" usually conjures up the image of a suicide bomber or terrorist. In the present context, the term is used more generally to refer to people who sacrifice their development or well-being for a principle or cause. In virtually every instance, the underlying issue is one involving dignity. Sometimes the dignity is their own, sometimes it's that of a group to which they belong. Sometimes others praise their acts, sometimes they condemn them. But invariably, martyrs see themselves as taking a stand against those who would deny their dignity.

From this broader perspective, martyrdom is seen to have many forms, not just the murderous, suicidal acts of terrorism that make the front page. It is a path that draws millions, not just the handful we read about. This broad, inclusive approach helps us understand why people choose martyrdom and what can be done to make any and all of its forms seem unattractive and unnecessary.

Martyrdom can be either active or passive. Passive martyrs repress the resentment that stems from lack of recognition and typically go unnoticed. They are prone to resignation, self-effacement, sometimes even self-destruction. Our schools are filled with students who opt out of learning rather than risk being stigmatized as "losers." For blacks this can mean resisting what they see as the "white way." For students in general it means refusing to do things the "right way," as held up to them by teachers and parents.

The reason so many pupils withhold their hearts and minds from what is being taught is that their first priority is to steel themselves against the indignities that beset our educational system from preschool on. The long-term consequences of doing this are often easier to bear than the brutal pain of derision. Society pays a terrible price for sponsoring institutions that force its young to make such tragic choices. Worse still is the fact that our schools merely reflect societal practices which force the same choice on adults.

In contrast to the passive martyrdom chosen by legions of students, active martyrs strike back at those they view as causing their torment. But despite their high visibility, they are only the tip of the iceberg. Below the waterline lie multitudes of passive martyrs resigned to deprivation and dissatisfaction. Though not willing to rebel openly like their activist comrades, they nonetheless usually sympathize with them.

The aftermath of an act of blatant terrorism often provides us with a glimpse of the full extent of passive martyrdom. In the weeks following the shootings at Columbine, thousands of school outcasts voiced complaints about intolerance, humiliation, and bullying. When an employee goes "postal," browbeaten workers from near and far, while distancing themselves from the violence, urge that their employers appoint ombudsmen. In the wake of the attacks of 9/11, thousands of disenfranchised young Muslims celebrated in the streets of foreign capitals.

The extent to which active martyrs depend on passive sympathizers for material and psychological support varies from one situation to the next. Not infrequently there are significant differences between the political motivations and goals of the activists and those who applaud their exploits. It is likely, for example, that many who regard themselves as supporters of Al Qaeda do not share either the specific political aims or the extreme antipathy for modernity and pluralism of its leadership. Sometimes all it takes to expose the divergence in goals between terrorists and their passive supporters is a visa to the West or a meaningful job at home.

But for there to be a renewable supply of suicide bombers, volunteers must feel they are acting on behalf of others subject to the same indignities who regard their martyrdom as a noble act. Most martyrs need to believe their sacrifice will not only bring recognition to themselves personally, but will draw attention to the indignities endured by an entire group to which they belong.

The American civil rights movement showed the world what happens when passive martyrs find a way to make their resentments known. For centuries the martyrdom of blacks took the form of stoic resignation to either slavery or menial jobs in a segregated, racist society. Protest had to remain covert — as in foot-dragging, sabotage, etc. — because more overt actions were summarily punished. In the 1960s, under the leadership of Dr. Martin Luther King, Jr., the Gandhian strategy of nonviolent civil disobedience gave millions of passive martyrs who were unwilling to perpetrate violence an acceptable way to become active martyrs. Thousands marched in the streets and subjected themselves to arrest and police brutality as the nation watched with mounting apprehension.

Any cause that can draw significant numbers of the countless passive martyrs out of their latency poses a grave threat to the status quo. As the ranks of nonviolent civil rights protestors swelled, Congress took steps to redress the injustices against which they were demonstrating. Faced with escalating disruption, Americans realized that evil lay not in the martyrs but in the racism that fueled their outrage, and began working to eliminate its degrading practices.

To combat terrorism societies must of course pursue and neutralize known perpetrators just as they do criminals. But the ultimate outcome of the struggle hinges on preventing a wholesale shift from passive to active martyrdom. We're unlikely to succeed in eradicating either domestic or international terrorism unless we alleviate the systemic indignities that depreciate lives and force people to choose between martyrdom and shame.

As it was in the sixties, so it is today: the suppression of active martyrs is not enough. We have to deal with the issue of passive martyrdom as well. At that time the root of the problem was racism — discrimination and exploitation based on race. Today it is "rankism" — discrimination and exploitation based on rank.

Rankism is abuse of the relatively weak and vulnerable by those who have higher rank and the superior power that comes with it. When rank is earned and exercised appropriately, people do not object to it. But when those of higher rank use their power for selfish or exploitative purposes, they provoke resentment. Rankism is *the* source of indignity and leads inevitably to indignation. Its perpetrators, in demeaning their victims, trigger recognition disorders, thereby ensuring a steady supply of willing martyrs.

The twentieth century is replete with horrific examples of the lengths to which individuals and nations will go in quest of pride and dignity. Time and again a humiliated people has heeded the call of a demagogic leader in hopes of establishing a new, more respected identity. A Nazi SS officer, reminiscing about German military victories in the early years of World War II, remarked, "It was with unrivaled pride that we saw the world. We were somebody."

The large-scale manifestations of recognition disorders that make news are like the periodic famines that draw our attention while chronic malnutrition, which leaves entire populations vulnerable to disease and death, goes unremarked. Left unaddressed, recognition deficiencies fester and eventually are writ large on the face of the world. If we wish to change this dynamic, we must first come to understand it. Why do people begrudge others recognition? Why do they persist in subjecting others to indignity?

At first it might be thought that our parsimony in dispensing recognition stems from legitimate doubts about the value of other people's contributions. But even when recognition is clearly merited, we're stinting with it — a sign that something else is at play. The explanation lies in our misguided hope that by withholding recognition from others we can keep potential competitors weak and thereby protect whatever prerogatives we enjoy by virtue of our present station.

Moral considerations aside, this strategy is short-sighted because as terrorist attacks have illustrated, some people value dignity above life itself. And most of us will seize the first opportunity to even the score with those who do not give us our due.

To reduce the incidence of nutritional deficiencies, we had to first determine what a healthy body needs and then take pains to ensure that everyone received enough of those vital nutrients. Although much remains to be done in both the developed and developing world, the 20th century witnessed significant progress toward ending malnutrition and eradicating hunger. For the first time in human history, it lies within our reach to end these scourges worldwide.

As proper food is necessary for our physical bodies, so is proper recognition for our psychological health and stability. As lack of proper food results in malnutrition, so lack of proper recognition results in what can be called "malrecognition."

Identifying and naming a problem is sometimes half the battle. Questions regarding the appropriate acknowledgment and compensation due the various ranks within our social and global institutions are now largely taboo. Making malrecognition visible and giving it priority is a vital first step.

The second step is to develop the taxonomy and science of recognition, which today are in their infancy. As was the case with malnutrition, a great deal of study will be needed to devise effective remedies for the various forms of malrecognition. One can imagine experts who focus on diagnosing and treating this problem — psychologists, diplomats and others whose specialty it is to spot symptoms of recognition deficiencies and work with individuals, institutions and nations to correct them before they assume the proportions of entrenched disorders.

Treating these maladies will require the understanding that in order to convey respect, recognition must be genuinely earned and given. Unless those acknowledged feel they have actually contributed something of value and thereby really deserve it, recognition just backfires. The condescension implicit in inflated praise feels patronizing and only exacerbates recognition deficiencies.

The way to a more equitable distribution of recognition is through authentic appreciation of the real value others create. As things stand now, when it comes to recognition, it's feast or famine. A few get the lion's share while a great many others must settle for crumbs.

But unlike the supply of food, that of recognition is unlimited. We don't have to disparage Peter in order to acknowledge Paul. To increase the supply of recognition we need only discern the varied contributions others make to the world and acknowledge them appropriately.

The difficulties involved in redistributing recognition without violence are great, but the costs of not doing so are far greater. Implementation will require ingenuity, perseverance, and patience. In the workplace it will mean that each person, from the boss to the janitor, must understand and respect the contributions of fellow employees and support a system of compensation that fairly acknowledges them. In the schools it means protecting the dignity of everyone, teachers and students alike, at every step in the learning process. We must stop using educational ranking as we have in the past — to effect and maintain a division between "winners" and "losers" and reconcile the latter to their station via humiliation and invalidation. Instead we must use testing exclusively and sensitively as a diagnostic tool that can help guide students towards specialization.

For conflicts between peoples or states, redistributing recognition means developing supranational institutions capable of taking a nonpartisan, comprehensive view of the legitimate interests of all parties and then mediating so that in the end everyone feels their concerns have received fair treatment.

Eliminating malrecognition is a task as daunting as ending world hunger. But the threat posed by malrecognition is even graver. Whereas malnutrition cripples individuals and occasionally rises to the level of famine, it is not contagious. In contrast, malrecognition spreads because when our dignity is offended, our first impulse is to do the same to others. Most alarmingly, the 20th century amply demonstrates that war, unlike famine, can leap easily and quickly from one continent to another.

Wherever there is domination, paternalism, harassment, ostracism, exploitation, territorial occupation or colonization — in short, wherever there is humiliation and indignity — there will be malrecognition and martyrdom. Passive resistance and violent outbursts in the workplace and schools, computer sabotage, terrorism, genocide and war all have their genesis in recognition disorders which in turn stem from systemic abrogations of people's dignity. Seeing these behaviors in such light does not excuse them any more than attributing a theft or murder to poverty excuses it. But this reframing does suggest a way to break dysfunctional patterns that now mar personal lives, cripple social institutions, threaten entire societies and preclude global peace.

The benefits of preventing malnutrition are now universally apparent. The effects of preventing malrecognition will be equally salutary. In a world where the few can hold the many hostage or threaten the health and security of the entire planet, there is no higher priority than the diagnosis and treatment of recognition disorders.

Memorandum: Building a Dignitarian Society

Purpose:

To suggest an analysis — complete with bumper stickers — that will galvanize victims of social injustice to voice and vote for their own political and economic self-interests.

Premise:

Social justice is never just handed to those who lack it. Only when the victims of unfairness are aroused and demand dignity and equity for themselves does the status quo change. Not until blacks found their voice and protested the injustice of racism did Americans outlaw segregationism. Not until women built the modern women's movement and targeted sexism were they able to win a measure of equity. What primarily marks people for mistreatment and exploitation today is not race or gender but low rank and the powerlessness it signifies. In plain language, what matters is whether you're a "somebody" or a "nobody."

Q: What do you mean by "somebody" and "nobody"?

A: Somebodies are the relatively powerful and successful, nobodies the relatively weak and vulnerable. Somebodies with higher rank and more power in any given context can maintain an environment that is hostile and demeaning to nobodies with lower rank and less power in that context, much as whites used to be at liberty to mistreat blacks and males were not obliged to treat females equitably. Taken together, those of low rank vastly outnumber those of high rank. They constitute a latent progressive majority.

Q: How can this majority be awakened?

A: The same way women were in the 1960s. They broke the taboo on discussing gender and initiated a process of consciousness-raising about gender issues. In the process they coined the term "sexism," which served to identify their grievances and proved instrumental in building the modern women's movement. In like manner, to transform the latent progressive majority into a political force, we must break the taboo on discussing rank, give a name to rank-based abuse and discrimination, and replace the prevailing social consensus that tacitly sanctions these practices with one that repudiates them.

Q: *What shall we call rank-based abuse and discrimination?*

A: When discrimination and injustice are race-based, we call it racism; when they're gender-based, we call it sexism. By analogy, rank-based abuse and exploitation can be called "rankism." As with any problem, we will not be able to overcome rankism unless we first identify, name, and call attention to it.

Q: *Are you proposing that we do away with rank?*

A: Not at all. When earned and exercised appropriately, rank is a legitimate, virtually indispensable tool of organization, and we rightly admire and respect those who attain it. But when those of higher rank *abuse* their authority, those of lower rank experience discrimination and injustice not different in their material and psychological effects from the discrimination and injustice we now disallow when their victims belong to the familiar identity groups. People do not object to differences in rank, only to abuses of those differences.

Q: *Why focus on rank instead of class?*

A: In modern democracies we interact with authority in terms of rank, not class. In contrast to aristocratic societies, in this society it does not matter whether your superior is a native or an immigrant, wealthy or not, white collar or blue. What matters is that he or she is your boss, your professor, your doctor, your commanding officer, your president.

Q: *What are the dynamics of rankism?*

A: Rankism occurs when rank-holders use the power of their position to secure unwarranted advantages or benefits for themselves. It typically takes the form of self-aggrandizement and exploitation of subordinates. It is the opposite of service. Good leaders eschew rankism; bad ones indulge in it. Since rankism is an impediment to meritocracy, overcoming it is a strategy for equalizing opportunity and securing social justice.

Q: *Where is rankism found?*

A: Any hierarchy is a breeding ground for rankism because hierarchies are built around rank and power. Thus, rankism can be found in government, corporations, businesses, workplaces, families, schools and universities, as well as religious, nonprofit, and healthcare organizations, and any other kind of bureaucracy. It also occurs at the global level between nations.

Q: *What are some of the effects of rankism?*

A: Rankism distorts personal relationships, erodes the will to work and to learn, taxes productivity, undermines public trust, fosters disease, stokes ethnic hatred and incites revenge. Current anti-Americanism is indicative of instances of international rankism just as the domestic racial protests of the 1960s were of American racism.

Q: *Who are the victims of rankism?*

A: Although racism and sexism target specific groups — primarily non-whites and females — we are all potential victims of rankism. This is because rank is not fixed, but relative. You can be a nobody in one context — and as such vulnerable to rankism — but a somebody in another — and thus a potential perpetrator. You can be a somebody one day and a nobody the next, increasing or decreasing your exposure to rank-based abuse overnight. Like racism in the era of segregation, rankism is pervasive and sanctioned by a tacit social consensus. And like the other "isms," it takes both interpersonal and institutional form.

Q: *What are some examples of interpersonal rankism?*

A: Examples of interpersonal rankism are a boss harassing an employee, a customer demeaning a waiter, a coach bullying a player, a doctor disparaging a nurse, a teacher humiliating a student, a parent belittling a child. The civil rights and women's movements have managed to put racists and sexists on notice. But there has been no corresponding outcry against rankist abuses that occur *within* a race or gender, in part because until now we haven't had a name for them. Blacks insult and exploit other blacks of lower rank, whites do the same to whites, and women to women, all with confidence that such behavior will pass for business as usual.

Q: *What are some examples of institutional rankism?*

A: Institutional rankism is the rankism we encounter when we deal with governments, corporations, hospitals, and other bureaucracies. In police states it takes the form of exploitation and oppression of the citizenry. In democracies it consists of the daily indignities of dealing with institutions whose de facto goal is self-preservation and aggrandizement rather than service. When bureaucratic, corporate or governmental corruption rises to the level of scandal, revulsion for institutional rankism can cause indignant shareholders or voters to turn against incumbents.

Q. *Who are the principal victims of institutional rankism today?*

A: In terms of the demographics of electoral politics, rankism afflicts no group more than the working poor. In *Nickel and Dimed: On (Not) Getting By in America*, Barbara Ehrenreich makes a compelling case that the working poor are in effect unacknowledged benefactors whose labor subsidizes those who are more advantaged. In *Wealth and Democracy: A Political History of the American Rich*, Kevin Phillips explores how the rich and politically powerful create and perpetuate privilege at the expense of the middle and lower classes. As described in the October 12, 2003 *New York Times Magazine* cover story, the chronic stress suffered by those of low socioeconomic status is a significant public health problem.

Q: *Everyone is sick of political correctness and "isms." Do we really need another?*

A: Yes, but it will be the last of the lot. For one thing, much of what is now labeled racism, sexism, etc. is actually not triggered by a difference in color, gender, or other such trait, but rather by a perception that the target lacks the protection of rank. It is rankism. Secondly, identity politics can foster resentment in those who feel that its concerns and protections don't extend to them. But no one is immune to rankism. Everyone has experienced it in some context or other (and most of us have dished it out). So overcoming rankism is a universal and unifying goal that reduces the myriad injunctions of political correctness to just one: Protect everyone's dignity equally.

Q: What would be the slogan — the bumper sticker — of a movement against rankism?

A: *End Rankism*, or just the single word *Rankism* with a diagonal line through it. Once there's a word for what galls them, people will use it to put their tormentors on the defensive, just as women used the label "sexist." Providing such a term has the benefit of shifting the burden of proof from victims to perpetrators.

Q: What exactly does the latent majority want?

A: A "dignitarian" society. People do not really want or expect an *egalitarian* society because everyone recognizes how different we all are. But they feel they have a right to equal dignity. As a central tenet of every religion, dignity would not be easy to campaign against.

Q: What does a dignitarian society look like? What are the policy implications?

A: At a minimum a dignitarian society means universal healthcare, equal access to quality education (including adult education and retraining), an equitable tax structure, affordable housing, and compensation compatible with living in dignity. The dignitarian framework encompasses all existing identity groups, spans old divisions, and takes aim at what still divides us — the dignity gap sustained by rankism. A dignitarian society embodies the promise our nation's founders imprinted on the national psyche — the right to both liberty *and* justice.

Q: *What are the political requirements for building a dignitarian society?*

A: Transforming a modern democracy into a significantly more equitable society requires the election of significant numbers of progressive legislators. It's hard to imagine this happening except in the context of national political realignment.

Q: *What would it take to effect national political realignment?*

A: Political realignment follows the success of any movement that overcomes the exploitation of one social group by another. The previously subordinated group shifts its support to the party that has championed its cause, whereas the previously dominant group takes refuge in the party that has defended the status quo. For example, the civil rights movement brought about political realignment as it overcame racism: African-Americans went Democratic and the South turned Republican. Likewise, the women's movement effected political realignment as it overcame sexism: women shifted to the Democratic Party while men moved to the Republican Party. As rankism is challenged and overcome, the beneficiaries will support the party that has fought on their behalf. In a dignitarian society, rank and file voters will not easily be persuaded to vote against their own economic interests in the name of defending the existing order.

Q: *A final statement?*

A: The road to social justice does not lead straight to equality; it passes first by way of dignity. Putting rankism on notice is a strategy for effecting political realignment. The idea, the goal of overcoming rankism and ending the dignity gap reframes democratic politics. A dignitarian society is democracy's next step.

EPILOGUE

The somebodies will be nobodies and
the nobodies will be somebodies.
 – Matthew 19:30 (trans. John Dominic Crossan)

When people ask what I do, I'm tempted to blurt out, "My name is Bob and I'm a nobody!" — at least while the stigma remains. I've come to think of myself as a home for identities. When incubating a new idea, I'm a nobody. When presenting it, I'm a somebody. Being a somebody is like taking a trip to the big city — exciting, but taxing. After a while it's nice to leave the commotion behind and go back to where I'm most comfortable and most alive.

I count this state of affairs as the biggest surprise of my life. Growing up, I always expected to be the same somebody for life, like my father. But by the time I was fifty I could look back and identify several distinct somebodies who had taken up residence within "me," and used me as a mouthpiece to argue one case or another. Now, a decade later, I see movements between somebody and nobody as a natural part of the life cycle of any contemporary questing person.

As for rankism, I think we've got it pegged. The fact that life isn't fair doesn't mean we have to be unfair to each other. We can now intercept the reflex to pass indignity down the line, and instead call it by name and disallow it. We don't want authority over others half so much as we want to avoid subservience ourselves. Equal dignity both suffices and satisfies.

From the merged vantage point of somebodies who know they are equally nobodies, domination and servility are repellent, insupportable and, like slavery, destined to become one of the embarrassments of the human story. Rankism contravenes a spiritual intuition that can be read on every page of that story: the equality of personhood and the sanctity of human dignity. Relegating rankism to the margins is at once a moral goal and a practical necessity in the twenty-first century.

ELEGY FOR NOBODIES

… Man is not Man as yet,
Nor shall I deem his object served, his end
Attained, his genuine strength put fairly forth,
While only here and there a star dispels
The darkness, here and there a towering mind
O'erlooks its prostrate fellows: when the host
Is out at once to the despair of night,
When all Mankind alike is perfected,
Equal in full-blown powers — then, not till then,
I say, begins Man's general infancy.

— Robert Browning, English poet (1812–89), from "Paracelsus"

EPITAPH FOR NOBODIES

All service ranks the same with God:
With God, whose puppets, best and worst,
Are we; there is no last nor first.

— Robert Browning, from "Pippa Passes"

RELATED READINGS

Some of the books listed here are included simply because they influenced me and I want to acknowledge my indebtedness to their authors. My annotations are not intended as summaries of the works cited, but rather as suggestions as to how they touch upon the themes in this book. Among the titles are ones that both underpin ideas in the book and elaborate its argument in various ways. The readings are listed, within categories, in the chronological order of their publication.

Fiction

Les Misérables, Victor Hugo (1862). Jean Valjean was a nobody who became a somebody who became a nobody who became immortal.

Diary of a Nobody, George & Weedon Grossmith (1888). These brothers may have invented the somebody-nobody distinction and, in so doing, turned themselves from nobodies into somebodies.

Master and Man, Leo Tolstoy (1895). A nobleman experiences the equality of human dignity as he makes the ultimate sacrifice.

Yertle the Turtle, Dr. Seuss (1950). Yertle, the Turtle King, loses the support of his terrapin tower.

Invisible Man, Ralph Ellison (1952). The kind of recognition that nourishes is recognition of our individuality, not recognition as a member of an identity group, be it racial or ideological.

The Death of Napoleon, Simon Leys (1986). A fable that explores the nobody within somebodies and the somebody within nobodies.

Memoir and Essay

A Room of One's Own, Virginia Woolf (1929). A feminist manifesto that demystifies genius.

Writing a Woman's Life, Carolyn Heilbrun (1988). Questing lives are no longer just for men.

Composing a Life, Mary Catherine Bateson (1989). Five women move out of Nobodyland.

Not Entitled, Frank Kermode (1995). Proceeding from its Shakespearian epigram ("He was a kind of nothing, titleless"), this memoir illuminates the process whereby identities evolve out of nothing, and how remembering their ephemeral nature only gains in importance as titles accumulate.

Living without a Goal, Jay Ogilvy (1995). Fashioning a life not in service to a goal but as a personal work of art.

Rank and Status

The Phenomenology of Mind, Georg Wilhelm Friedrich Hegel (1806) or *Introduction to the Reading of Hegel*, Alexandre Kojeve (paperback, 1980). The dialectic between master and slave, to which all subsequent analyses of the politics of recognition are indebted.

The Outsider, Colin Wilson (1956). Many of the outsiders in this book were nobodies who forced the world to beat a path to their doors. A later age dubbed them, collectively, the counterculture.

The Presentation of Self in Everyday Life (1959) and *Stigma: Notes on the Management of a Spoiled Identity* (paperback, 1986), Erving Goffman. Public personas are carapaces to protect against insult; energy spent warding off indignity is energy unavailable for getting the job done; the goal of the stigmatized person is to gain the respect and regard he or she would receive but for the stigma.

The Other America, Michael Harrington (1962). Classic account of America's working poor.

The Hidden Injuries of Class, Richard Sennett and Jonathan Cobb (1972, rev. 1993). The ins and outs of Nobodyland.

The Denial of Death, Ernest Becker (1973). Disenthralling ourselves from the "spell cast by persons."

Class: A Guide Through the American Status System, Paul Fussell (1983). Delineates nine rungs on the ladder of class (social rank).

Choosing the Right Pond: Human Behavior and the Quest for Status, Robert H. Frank (1985). Why do we feel driven to achieve high rank in the social hierarchies we belong to?

The Saturated Self: Dilemmas of Identity in Contemporary Life, Kenneth J. Gergen (1991). The building blocks of a post-modern identity, in words and images.

The Winner-Take-All Society: Why the Few at the Top Get So Much More Than the Rest of Us, Robert H. Frank and Philip J. Cook (1995). The warping of public life by the domination of a few big winners and the existence of many losers.

Scorpion Tongues: Gossip, Celebrity and American Politics, Gail Collins (1998). Gossip, by dispelling the somebody mystique, changes the balance of power between somebodies and nobodies.

Respect: An Exploration, Sara Lawrence-Lightfoot (1999). Respect is a many-splendored way to create symmetry, empathy, and connection.

The Paradox of Success: When Winning at Work Means Losing at Life: A Book of Renewal for Leaders, John O'Neil (paperback, 2000). A guidebook for how to be successful in life as well as in work.

In the Name of Identity: Violence and the Need to Belong, Amin Maalouf (2001). Identity is often formed in relation to groups we fear or resent. Humiliation creates "identities that kill."

At the Hands of Persons Unknown: The Lynching of Black America, Philip Dray (2002). Only lynching and torture top slavery in rankism's chamber of horrors.

Snobbery: The American Version, Joseph Epstein (2002). The essence of snobbery is arranging to make yourself feel superior at the expense of other people.

Women's Inhumanity to Woman, Phyllis Chesler (2002). Overcoming sexism does not mean we have overcome rankism.

Identity Politics

Anti-Semite and Jew: An Exploration of the Etiology of Hate, Jean-Paul Sartre (1948). Excavating the roots of racial prejudice and xenophobia.

The Second Sex, Simone de Beauvoir (1949). The beginning of the end of modern sexism. "One is not born a woman, one becomes one."

The Feminine Mystique, Betty Friedan (1963). Triggered the modern women's movement by demystifying sex roles.

The Dialectic of Sex, Shulamith Firestone (1970). Patriarchy and the gender-based class system.

Imperial Middle: Why Americans Can't Think Straight About Class, Benjamin DeMott (1990). Demolishes the myth that America is a classless society.

Philosophical Arguments, Charles Taylor (1995) and *Multiculturalism: Examining the Politics of Recognition*, Charles Taylor, K. Anthony Appiah, Jürgen Habermas, Steven Rockefeller, Michael Walzer, and Susan Wolf; Amy Gutmann, ed. (1994). The politics of recognition and equal dignity made as clear and compelling as Euclid made geometry.

The Next American Nation: The New Nationalism and the Fourth American Revolution, Michael Lind (1995). The emergence of a multiracial, middle-class American majority heralds a post-identity group politics.

Color Conscious: The Political Morality of Race, Amy Gutmann and Kwame Anthony Appiah (1996). To what extent is race trumped by rank?

The Futures of Women: Scenarios for the 21st Century, Pamela McCorduck and Nancy Ramsey (1997). Four scenarios for women's lives across the globe over the next 20 years, ranging from virtual slavery to liberation, and from stagnation to separatism.

Out for Good: The Struggle to Build a Gay Rights Movement in America, Dudley Clendinen and Adam Nagourney (1999). Dramatic history of the twentieth century's most recent civil rights movement.

Self, Identity, and Social Movements, Sheldon Stryker, Timothy J. Owens, and Robert W. White, eds. (2000). A psychological view of social movements.

Doing Democracy: The MAP Model for Organizing Social Movements, Bill Moyer with JoAnn McAllister, Mary Lou Finley, and Steven Soifer (2001). A model of the eight stages through which social movements evolve and the four roles that activists play in fostering social change.

Up From Invisibility: Lesbians, Gay Men, and the Media in America, Larry Gross (2002). The mass media's relationship to homosexuality from mid-century to the present day.

Making Gay History: The Half-Century Fight for Lesbian and Gay Equal Rights, Eric Marcus (2002). Illuminates a history of the movement with 60 "personal is political" stories.

Brown: The Last Discovery of America, Richard Rodriguez (2002). Life in the "brown" postmodern mélange that is gradually supplanting identity politics.

Liberty, Equality, and Justice

Democracy in America, Alexis de Tocqueville (1835–40). Observed the American trend toward equality, and predicted it would be irreversible.

Two Cheers for Democracy, E. M. Forster (1938). "One [cheer] because it admits variety and two because it permits criticism." Could a dignitarian movement earn the third cheer — for fraternity — that Forster withheld?

The Opium of the Intellectuals, Raymond Aron (1955). Deconstruction of the left-right divide in European politics.

Two Concepts of Liberty, Isaiah Berlin (1958). Elucidates the trade-offs between freedom, liberty, justice, dignity, and equality. *Two Faces of Liberalism*, John Gray (1999) tackles the same issues.

Strong Democracy, Benjamin R. Barber (1984). The cure for the ills of democracy is more democracy—not only in politics, but in other civil institutions.

Lincoln at Gettysburg: The Words that Remade America, Garry Wills (1992). By invoking Jefferson's "All are created equal" at Gettysburg, Lincoln asserted the equality of the races.

The End of Equality, Mickey Kaus (1992). "Civic liberalism," emphasizing not financial equality but social equality, as the path to justice.

Moral Politics: What Conservatives Know that Liberals Don't, George Lakoff (1996). Linguistic deconstruction of American partisan politics.

Achieving Our Country: Leftist Thought in Twentieth-Century America, Richard Rorty (1998). Rehabilitating our democratic institutions to achieve social justice.

The Story of American Freedom, Eric Foner (1998). The long and winding road toward freedom and justice in America.

On Democracy, Robert A. Dahl (1999). The perennial struggle to find equality within democracy.

Natural Capitalism: Creating the Next Industrial Revolution, Paul Hawken, Amory Lovins, and L. Hunter Lovins (1999). If capitalism were shorn of rankism, it would bear a striking resemblance to this book's "natural capitalism."

The Right to Vote: The Contested History of Democracy in the United States, Alex Keyssar (2000). Democracy's mantra—one man, one vote—is not as straightforward as it may seem.

The Radical Center: The Future of American Politics, Ted Halstead and Michael Lind (2001). Imagining a new politics beyond the old categories of right and left.

Wealth and Democracy, Kevin Phillips (2002). A reminder of the gap between Jefferson's "All are created equal" and the current reality, wherein the U. S. is "home to greater economic inequality than any other Western nation." Is American democracy becoming a plutocracy?

The Best Democracy Money Can Buy, Greg Palast (2002). The corrupting influence of big money on American democracy.

Etiquette and Manners

Rudeness and Civility, John F. Kasson (1990). Manners encode civility, but "Established codes of behavior have often served in unacknowledged ways as checks against a fully democratic order."

Miss Manners Rescues Civilization, Judith Martin (1996). The title hints at the connection between rankism, indignity, indignation, and violence.

Civility: Manners, Morals, and the Etiquette of Democracy, Stephen Carter (1998). Civility is understood as disciplining our passions for the sake of living a common life with others, as welcoming the stranger without trying to make an enemy or a brother out of everyone.

A Short History of Rudeness: Manners, Morals, and Misbehavior in Modern America, Mark Caldwell (2001). Do manners within hierarchies support or suppress abuses of rank, or both?

Choosing Civility: The Twenty-Five Rules of Considerate Conduct, P. M. Forni (2002). How civility affects the quality of life in the workplace and in society at large.

Rankism in the Workplace

Bully in Sight: How to Predict, Resist, Challenge and Combat Workplace Bullying, Tim Field (1996). Written with the experience and insight that only a onetime target can impart. Details the injury to health caused by stress resulting from bullying and harassment.

Work Abuse: How to Recognize and Survive It, Chauncey Hare and Judith Wyatt (1997). Profound, pioneering work that delivers on the brave promise—survive!—of its title.
Website <http://home.netcom.com/~workfam1/>.

Working: People Talk About What They Do All Day and How They Feel About What They Do, Studs Terkel (paperback, 1997). Classic depiction of the lives of workers, in their own words.

Living Wage: Building a Fair Economy, Robert Pollin and Stephanie Luce (1998). The basic text of the living wage movement.

Mobbing: Emotional Abuse in the American Workplace, Noa Davenport, Ruth Distler Schwartz, and Gail Pursell Elliott (1999). A safety manual for avoiding the dignity-robbing trauma of being ganged up on by co-workers.
Website <http://mobbing-usa.com>.

The Working Class Majority: America's Best Kept Secret, Michael Zweig (2000). Sees class not as wealth, but as power, i.e., as rank in a social hierarchy.

Nickel and Dimed: On (Not) Getting By in America, Barbara Ehrenreich
(2001). Holding a succession of subsistence level jobs, the author
chronicles the daily struggle of the working poor, and concludes that
they are unacknowledged benefactors whose work effectively
subsidizes everyone else.

Good to Great: Why Some Companies Make the Leap…and Others Don't,
Jim Collins (2001). Great companies are inhospitable to rankism.

Rankism in Education

The Rise of the Meritocracy, Michael Young (1958). Introduced the word
"meritocracy" as a pejorative, arguing that basing advancement on
educational testing instead of inheritance would skim the cream off
the working class, denude it of leadership, and thus damage the
cause of social justice.

Summerhill: A Radical Approach to Child Rearing, A.S. Neill (1960).
The transformation of teaching from domination to exemplification.
(As a young schoolteacher in Scotland, Neill bore the intimidating
title "dominie.")

Excellence: Can We Be Equal and Excellent Too? John Gardner (1961,
rev. 1995). The title is one of those pregnant questions that suggests
its own answer.

Pedagogy of the Oppressed, Paulo Freire (1980). The connection between
learning and the power relationships that shape it at every turn.

Savage Inequalities: Children in America's Schools, Jonathan Kozol
(1991). The toll taken by rankist schools.

You Can't Say You Can't Play, Vivian Paley (1992). Nipping rankism in
the bud.

An Aristocracy of Everyone, Benjamin R. Barber (1992). Democratizing education.

The Big Test: The Secret History of the American Meritocracy, Nicholas Lemann (1999). A key instrument of American meritocracy—the S.A.T.—fails to apportion opportunity equally and fairly: "You can't undermine social rank by setting up an elaborate process of ranking."

Nobody Left to Hate: Teaching Compassion after Columbine, Elliot Aronson (2000). A social psychological perspective on bullying, humiliation, and exclusion in schools.

Schools That Learn, Peter Senge, ed. (2000). An overview of the transformation required of schools in postindustrial, knowledge-based societies.

Tomorrow's Children: A Blueprint for Partnership Education for the 21st Century, Riane Eisler (paperback, 2001). A blueprint for the participatory, proactive education children will need to flourish in knowledge-based economies.

Mom, They're Teasing Me: Helping Your Child Solve Social Problems, Michael Thompson, Lawrence J. Cohen, and Catherine O'Neill Grace (2002). The stereotype of the school bully is outmoded: nowadays, social cruelty is more likely to come from kids with social power than those with brute strength.

International Politics and Human Rights

Theory of International Politics, Kenneth Waltz (1979). The dominant paradigm for the study of power and security among nation-states.

Jihad vs. McWorld, Benjamin R. Barber (1995). Democratizing the international economy and global institutions.

Democracy at Risk: Rescuing Main Street from Wall Street, Jeff Gates (2000). A passionate, fact-laden, and rigorous argument from the architect of the legislation that created ESOPs (employee stock ownership plans) for sharing capital in the name of building a fully functioning democracy.

The Future of International Human Rights: Commemorating the 50th Anniversary of the Universal Declaration of Human Rights, Burns H. Weston, ed. (2000). Assesses the legacy of the Universal Declaration, and explores the viable pathways to the future that it opens up.

The Shadow of the Sun, Ryszard Kapuscinski (2001). Indignities of third world life.

Empire, Michael Hardt and Antonio Negri (2001). The supranational order presiding over globalization lacks the democratic mechanisms that give representation to the citizens of democratic nation-states. Protesters are not necessarily against globalization, but they are for the democratization of globalizing processes.

"The US and International Organizations," Stanley Hoffman in *Eagle Rules? Foreign Policy and American Primacy in the Twenty-First Century,* Robert J. Lieber, ed. (2001). Hoffman's term "bossism"— the use of international and regional institutions to impose American views—gives an evocative name to the humiliations of international rankism.

Human Rights as Politics and Idolatry, Michael Ignatieff et al. (2001). Deep questions about the future of human rights.

Sovereign Virtue: The Theory and Practice of Equality, Ronald Dworkin (2002). Argues that politics should place the pursuit of equality over the pursuit of liberty; that persistent inequality reflects the fact that the wealthy can buy the political influence that shields their ranks from fair competition.

The Paradox of American Power: Why the World's Only Superpower Can't Go It Alone, Joseph S. Nye, Jr. (2002). The loneliness of the long-distance superpower.

Global Women: Nannies, Maids, and Sex Workers in the New Economy, Barbara Ehrenreich and Arlie Hochschild, eds. (2002). The migrant nanny—or cleaning woman, nursing care attendant, maid—eases a "care deficit" in rich countries, while her absence creates a care deficit back home. This anthology reveals that the main resource extracted from the third world is no longer gold or silver, but love.

Rich Democracies: Political Economy, Public Policy and Performance, Harold L. Wilensky (2002). An empirical, comparative study showing that participatory decision-making serves a nation's citizens better than confrontation, and shedding light on the likely paths of development of rich democracies as they become richer.

A Time for Choices: Deep Dialogues for Deep Democracy, Michael Toms, ed. (2002). A collection of interviews conducted in the aftermath of September 11 on New Dimensions Radio with a diverse group of people. My piece provides kernels of the present book, locating the solution to terrorism in overcoming the rankism, recognition disorders, and dignity-indignity gaps that lie at its roots.

Longitudes and Attitudes: Exploring the World after September 11, Thomas Friedman (2002). What we must do and, equally, what others must do to avoid an unnecessary clash of civilizations.

War Is A Force That Gives Us Meaning, Chris Hedges (2002). The days when national identity could be forged in war are behind us. We must and we can learn a "better game."

Humiliation: A New Basis for Understanding, Preventing, and Defusing Conflict and Violence in the World and Our Lives, Evelin Gerda Linder (2003). An examination into the etiology of violence, reminiscent of Sartre's explorations into the etiology of hate. The humiliation that individuals and states inflict on each other come back to haunt them. Available free to download at <www.humiliationstudies.org>.

Overviews

Homo Ludens: A Study of the Play Element in Culture, Johan Huizinga (1950). Is Man Homo sapiens (the wise), Homo faber (the maker), or Homo ludens (the player)? Or, is Man Homo modulus (the modeler), capable of distinguishing between proper and improper uses of power, and disallowing those that do net harm? That is, will Homo modulus overcome rankism?

Crowds and Power, Elias Canetti (1960). Somebodies "sting" nobodies, who displace the insult onto those who are nobodies to *them*.

Natural Law and Human Dignity, Ernst Bloch (German, 1961; English paperback, 1986). Upholds the ideals of liberty, equality, and fraternity—"a tradition that has not yet become"—against all forms of tyranny.

A Theory of Justice, John Rawls (1971, rev. 1999). Classic treatment of justice as fairness. "Each person possesses an inviolability founded on justice that even the welfare of society as a whole cannot override."

Spheres of Justice: A Defense of Pluralism and Equality, Michael Walzer (1983). Illuminates the path to social justice.

The End of History and The Last Man, Francis Fukuyama (1992). Democracy's "long march" to preeminence.

The Good Society: The Humane Agenda, John Kenneth Galbraith (1996). Provides an answer to its question, "The tragic gap between the fortunate and the needful having been recognized, how can it be closed?"

The Decent Society, Avishai Margalit (1996). A "decent" society is a dignity-respecting society — that is, one that disallows institutional humiliation of the weak.

Inequality Reexamined (1996) and *Development as Freedom* (1999), Amartya Sen. Development economics that transcends left-right politics.

On Beauty and Being Just, Elaine Scarry (1999). The symmetries of art (e.g., symmetry as beauty), of nature (e.g., invariance principles of physics), and of everyone's relation to one another (e.g., Rawls's principles of justice) are connected.

Nonzero: The Logic of Human Destiny, Robert Wright (2000). Right makes might, not vice versa.

The Power of Partnership: The Seven Relationships That Will Change Your Life, Riane Eisler (2002). By the author of the bestseller *The Chalice and the Blade* (1987), this practical handbook tells how to move from control and domination to respectful partnership in personal relationships, workplaces, organizations and communities.

Websites Related to Rankism

<http://breakingranks.net>

<www.dignitarians.org>

<www.humiliationstudies.org>

<http://worktrauma.org>

<www.successunlimited.co.uk>

<http://workplacebullying.co.uk>

<http://workdoctor.com>.

<http://planetearthfdn.org>

<http://workingwounded.com>

Nineveh Yahoo forum on workplace bullying
    <groups.yahoo.com/group/Nineveh>

ACKNOWLEDGMENTS

We are all products of the assistance we can accept.
  — I. A. Richards

I have been assisted by so many people, in so many different ways, that detailing all my debts is impossible. The names of some who have contributed can be found on the website <breakingranks.net> which, since its creation in March 2000 by webmaster Melanie Hart, has served as a forum for the ideas in this book and a place where people could tell their stories.

Mentors who transmitted the framework and seeded the questions that shape the analysis include my parents, Calvin S. and Willmine W. Fuller; my thesis professor John A. Wheeler; and philosopher Peter A. Putnam.

Indispensable feedback — in life and on the page — was provided by family members Ann, Karen, and Benjamin Fuller; Alia and Noah Johnson and Adam Fuller; and Stephen and John Fuller.

Among the many friends, teachers, and colleagues who left their mark on this work are Eric Best, Chuck Blitz, Jennifer Bloomfield, Keith Blume, Peter Budlong, Nick Burgoyne, Fred Byron, Jr., Napier Collyns, Bill Davis, Dominic DiLorenzo, Emma Edwards, Judd Fermi, David Ford, Peter Funkhouser, Steve Gillman, Daniel A. Greenberg, Jay Greenberg, Wade Greene, Chauncey Hare, John Harris, David Hoffman, Charles Huey, David Hunter, Tony Husch, Todd Johnston, Kevin Kelly, Jean Klein, Art Kleiner, Jennifer Ladd, Ted Lockwood, David Love, Jacqueline Lowell, Bob Mazer, Evelyn Messinger, David Michaelis, Bill

Moyer, Jay Ogilvy, John O'Neil, Fran Peavey, Delia Pitts, I. I. Rabi, Mel Randall, Hasan Schahbaz, Lynn Schwenger, Jack Scott, Thaddeus Sheridan, Gordon Sherman, Joan Stepp Smith, Mark Sommer, Kim Spencer, Edwin Taylor, Gail Taylor, David Thomas, Oliver Van Cise, F. Champion Ward, Catherine Webb, Toby Wells, Jack Willis, Mary Willis, and Mike Wollenberg.

I also wish to acknowledge Donald Reich, formerly Professor of Government at Oberlin College, for validating this line of inquiry at its inception; Stewart Brand and Ryan Phelan, for grasping the idea and backing me; David Landau, for elucidating the historical context and, time and again, offering wise editorial counsel; Michael and Justine Toms, for providing me a forum on New Dimensions Radio; Sandy Close, for syndicating op-eds on rankism through Pacific News Service; Katherine Fulton, Roberta Gelt, Nancy Murphy, and Peter Schwartz at Global Business Network for offering opportunities to present my ideas to the public; and Janet Coleman, for her structural editing and for publishing an extended excerpt from the manuscript in The Peter Drucker Foundation's quarterly magazine *Leader to Leader*.

At New Society Publishers, the book has rested in the caring and capable hands of Chris and Judith Plant, Justine Johnson, Heather Wardle, Sue Custance and Ingrid Witvoet. Diane McIntosh created the striking and evocative cover.

When it comes to challenging a social consensus, the provocation of critics is as important as the encouragement of supporters. Recognition is therefore due to the agents, editors, publishers and visitors to the website whose critiques, questions and comments forced me to elaborate and sharpen my analysis.

Three friends who have been intimately involved in every phase of this undertaking are Thomas Purvis, witness and participant from kindergarten on to many of the formative incidents recounted herein; John Hobbs, who, as my writing coach, saw the book through all its incarnations; and John Steiner, whose support was unconditional from first to last.

Editorial assistance was provided by Guy Croyle, Janet Kastelic, Zara Wallace and Ina Cooper, who lent her extraordinary abilities to the project during its final stages.

The book is dedicated to Robert Cabot, whose trust made it possible.

For her unerring judgment, her uncompromising integrity, and her unwavering heart, my deep and abiding gratitude to my wife, Claire Sheridan.

INDEX

About the Author

ROBERT W. FULLER

Robert Fuller has had three distinct careers in as many decades. After attending Oberlin College and getting a Ph.D. in physics from Princeton University, he taught physics at Columbia University in New York City.

While authoring a book on mathematical physics at the Battelle Seattle Research Center, he started a course for dropouts in a local high school and began writing about education. This led him back to academia and to the presidency of his alma mater, Oberlin College. His second career consisted of leading Oberlin through a series of educational reforms, many of which drew national attention.

After this, Fuller traveled extensively, coming to rest in California, where a third career took shape in the movement which came to be known during the Cold War as "citizen diplomacy." This involves individuals or small groups taking personal initiative in establishing relationships with people in other countries to bridge the gaps in understanding that often breed hostility. As Fuller says, "International diplomacy is too important to be left exclusively to professionals. Private citizens must take responsibility for creating peace and justice themselves." He thinks of this work as "a better game than war," and it has taken him to Russia, China, India, South Africa, the Middle East, South America, Vietnam, Afghanistan, Somalia, and Bosnia.

Fuller long served as Board Chair of the nonprofit global corporation Internews, which promotes democracy and international understanding via free and independent media. In 1999 Internews helped launch WorldLink TV, the first international public affairs channel for Americans.

A contributor in a range of disciplines to magazines including *Harvard Magazine*, *The Utne Reader*, *Whole Earth Review*, and the Peter Drucker Foundation's *Leader to Leader*, Fuller is also co-author of the classic text *Mathematics for Classical and Quantum Physics*. Beginning in 1997, the Pacific News Service has syndicated several op-eds by him on "rankism" — the central notion in *Somebodies and Nobodies: Overcoming the Abuse of Rank*.

Robert Fuller has four children and lives in Berkeley, California with his wife, Claire Sheridan.

If you have enjoyed *Somebodies and Nobodies*,
you might also enjoy other

BOOKS TO BUILD A NEW SOCIETY

Our books provide positive solutions for people who want to
make a difference. We specialize in:

Sustainable Living • Ecological Design and Planning
Natural Building & Appropriate Technology • New Forestry
Environment and Justice • Conscientious Commerce
Progressive Leadership • Resistance and Community • Nonviolence
Educational and Parenting Resources

New Society Publishers

ENVIRONMENTAL BENEFITS STATEMENT

New Society Publishers has chosen to produce this book on New Leaf EcoBook
100, recycled paper made with 100% post consumer waste, processed chlorine
free, and old growth free.

For every 5,000 books printed, New Society saves the following resources:[1]

25	Trees
2,283	Pounds of Solid Waste
2,512	Gallons of Water
3,276	Kilowatt Hours of Electricity
4,150	Pounds of Greenhouse Gases
18	Pounds of HAPs, VOCs, and AOX Combined
6	Cubic Yards of Landfill Space

[1]Environmental benefits are calculated based on research done by the Environmental Defense Fund
and other members of the Paper Task Force who study the environmental impacts of the paper
industry.

For more information on this environmental benefits statement, or to inquire about environmentally
friendly papers, please contact New Leaf Paper – info@newleafpaper.com Tel: 888 • 989 • 5323.

For a full list of NSP's titles, please call 1-800-567-6772 *or check out our web site at:*

www.newsociety.com

NEW SOCIETY PUBLISHERS

Our books provide positive solutions for people who want to make a difference.

❑ Please mail me a hard copy of your catalog.

Please notify me via email as new resources become available
in the following area/s of interest:

❑ Making a Difference
❑ Sustainable Living
❑ New Economics
❑ Conscientious Commerce
❑ ProgressiveLeadership
❑ Organizational Devt.

❑ Ecological Design and Planning
❑ Sustainable Transportation
❑ New Forestry
❑ Educational & Parenting Resources
❑ Education for Sustainability
❑ All of the above

Name_____

Address/City/Province_____

Postal Code/Zip_____ Email Address_____

800-567-6772

NEW SOCIETY PUBLISHERS

www.newsociety.com

NEW SOCIETY PUBLISHERS
P.O. Box 189
Gabriola Island, B.C.
V0R 1X0
CANADA

BOOKS TO BUILD A NEW SOCIETY

Place
Postage
Here